FREQUENCY™ MATTERS

Be a Contributor, Not an Employee!

Kristin Mackey and Shawn Herbig

Illustrations by Kristin Mackey

BALBOA.
PRESS
A DIVISION OF HAY HOUSE

Copyright © 2017 Kristin M. Mackey-DiObilda and Shawn Herbig.
FREQUENCY MATTERS™ is a trademark of Kristin Mackey-DiObilda.

All rights reserved. No part of this book may be used or reproduced by any means, graphic, electronic, or mechanical, including photocopying, recording, taping or by any information storage retrieval system without the written permission of the author except in the case of brief quotations embodied in critical articles and reviews.

Balboa Press books may be ordered through booksellers or by contacting:

Balboa Press
A Division of Hay House
1663 Liberty Drive
Bloomington, IN 47403
www.balboapress.com
1 (877) 407-4847

Because of the dynamic nature of the Internet, any web addresses or links contained in this book may have changed since publication and may no longer be valid. The views expressed in this work are solely those of the author and do not necessarily reflect the views of the publisher, and the publisher hereby disclaims any responsibility for them.

The author of this book does not dispense medical advice or prescribe the use of any technique as a form of treatment for physical, emotional, or medical problems without the advice of a physician, either directly or indirectly. The intent of the author is only to offer information of a general nature to help you in your quest for emotional and spiritual well-being. In the event you use any of the information in this book for yourself, which is your constitutional right, the author and the publisher assume no responsibility for your actions.

Any people depicted in stock imagery provided by Thinkstock are models, and such images are being used for illustrative purposes only. Certain stock imagery © Thinkstock.

Print information available on the last page.

ISBN: 978-1-5043-3291-0 (sc)
ISBN: 978-1-5043-3293-4 (hc)
ISBN: 978-1-5043-3292-7 (e)

Library of Congress Control Number: 2017909783

Balboa Press rev. date: 07/24/2017

This book is dedicated to
William C. Mackey and **Barbara Mackey**.

Thank you for your love, your generosity and joyful spirits. I am sincerely grateful for the arena you provided so that I might find and express
my own unique frequency.

I love you.

This book is dedicated to you.

Love, Kristin

In loving memory of John M. Sanders, a mentor.

AUTHORS' NOTE

Two authors worked together harmoniously on this book. Sometimes you will hear from Kristin; sometimes from Shawn. In many areas, you will draw from both. You will also hear the stories, paths, tidbits and wisdom of inspiring leaders.

Some contributors lead teams and organizations down remarkable paths as they win awards, new business and athletic games or forge strong family connections and friends. Others have mastered a resilient body, clear mind or grateful heart.

It is up to you to decide which ideas resonate and which do not.

Their presence in this material does not reflect the author's opinions. Their participation is intended to inspire, offer varied ideas and showcase the diverse paths to wellbeing, happiness and success.

Enjoy the team experience, take notes in the back and make this book a little reminder that our frequencies matter.

We can be different. We can harmonize. We can succeed.

FOREWORD

When I first sat down to write this foreword, I was planning to go into all-out cheerleader mode. I was going to tell you why this book is so great, how authentic the stories are, and how the graphics make the subject matter approachable.

While all of those things are true, I want to step back and tell you a little bit about why I think you should take time now to learn from these leaders and why this book is so important today.

All leaders aspire to reach their personal potential and all great team members aspire to be part of a great team. Some would suggest that the desire to be a part of "something bigger than yourself" is stronger now than it has ever been.

But, how do you get there?

No, seriously. How do you get there?

It's not an easy question, and let's be honest, you wouldn't be reading this book if you weren't already 1) on the path and 2) realizing that the path is hard.

When Kristin and I first met, we were working to improve the team member engagement scores for a resort hotel in Miami. This was an iconic property that was already performing well, and they wanted their 2,000 team members to truly reach excellence.

Our personalities were completely opposite, but we connected instantly on our mutual goal. Her energy and optimism were a great counter-balance when I had to deliver tough results and have candid conversations.

You'll hear more about our work later in the book, so let's just say that when you are trying to get 2,000 people to their highest potential, you need more than hyperbole.

What we needed then is what all leaders need today. You need to have the proper mindset and you need to understand the landscape. You also need to define your ideal team culture – knowing what you are looking for and what you will contribute. Only then can you begin to put the pieces together and create a path towards excellence.

In other words, you need to find your frequency and that of your team to get everyone on the same page.

The diverse voices in this book belong to college coaches, business executives and organizational leaders. They are practitioners with deep knowledge and players with real experience. Combined, they bring you their insights and experiences as well as those from the hundreds and thousands of individuals and organizations with whom they have worked in the past.

This culminates into a full team of people who want nothing more than to see you succeed!

To get the most out of this book, you will need to be an active participant. As you hear from these leaders you are encouraged to pick up those pieces that most strongly resonate for you, but feel free to leave behind anything that does not fit. Then, by weaving those pieces together you can create your path forward.

You can find your alignment – your frequency – and spread that to others.

I have been working in research and data analytics since the mid 1990s. I began my career with Ford Motor Company, then started my own research firm at the age of 28. Over the last 18 years, my company has developed nationally recognized research in the healthcare, automotive and transportation sectors. In that same time, I've had the privilege of working with thousands of professionals from multiple industries and continents.

I am confident when I tell you that Kristin's work is unique. She makes the material approachable and fun so that you – the reader – can get the most from the experience and enjoy the journey.

Take this step to continue your path of excellence. Use this book to accomplish your ambitions. Let the experiences and philosophies of this book's contributors guide your path to engagement.

Welcome to the journey.

Shawn Herbig
President
IQS Research

PREFACE

An article in **Gallup** (Mann, Annamarie and Harter, Jim, "The Worldwide Employee Engagement Crisis", January 7, 2016: 5) stated:

"The world has an employee engagement crisis, with serious and potentially lasting repercussions for the global economy."

Looking at the countless studies reported by **Gallup** over the years, it is clear that if you want to increase revenue, reduce errors, raise customer satisfaction and lower employee turnover (and reap the benefits of high performance), you've got to tap into the positive and measurable impact of employee engagement.

Employee engagement is both an art and a science. Developing an understanding of our essential human needs is an effective recipe for sustaining a highly engaged organization, team or family.

With 87% of the world's employees unengaged, we need a fresh approach.

> *The problem always comes with the solution.*
> *How far are you willing to go to see it?*
> *More importantly, how will you respond once you do?*

A good question to ask yourself is:

WHAT IGNITES YOUR PASSION?

I "officially" began my public speaking career in 1997. I started by submitting a video to a business seminar company and was contacted to fly out to Kansas City for a week-long interview. One week before the start date, I was in a car accident that totaled my car. The topic I was to teach? Stress Management. I was 25.

While in Kansas, I stayed focused, practiced and delivered my program with energy and enthusiasm (and far too many hand gestures). I eliminated the gestures swiftly after receiving the feedback from a single group viewing.

I was hired.

Following the good news, those of us who had been hired decided to go downtown for lunch and unwind after such intensive interviews. We wanted to celebrate. As we walked the streets of Kansas City, we passed a homeless man asking for spare change.

As we approached him, his eager eyes turned sullen. My new colleagues had muttered "get a job" as they passed.

My heart sank. I tried to hand over the loose $5 bill I had.

With one backward swoop, my new work "friend" grabbed it playfully from my hand, laughing the word "Don't!" though it was neither funny nor informative. As we continued walking, it set in more and more that this outcome did not resonate with me.

I soon realized (after some internal pontification) that I had not made that decision; it was made for me. I then asked myself, "Why did I let this person (or situation) hijack what I felt was the right choice *for me?*"

So I stopped walking, told the group I would meet up later and went back to the homeless man to help him out. After receiving the $5, the man appeared grateful, his dignity restored. He mattered. He had value.

And although it was not anyone's responsibility to give him change, nor was anyone "wrong" for not doing so, it was *my choice*. It felt on target.

As I wandered the city, feeling whole on the inside but slightly dissonant on the outside, my eyes caught a little bookstore across the street. Instant lift.

I crossed at the light, walked straight to the back of the store and spotted a gold book with the word "Workbook" printed on the spine. I'm an unapologetic fan of workbooks. Paper workbooks. This particular workbook was the **Handbook to Higher Consciousness Workbook, The Science of Happiness** by Ken Keyes, Jr., and I was instantly delighted by this surprise find. I devoured every page and practice . . . *for the next 20 years*.

That moment with the homeless man became a defining one for me. It became the diversion that kept me ON track, not off.

Since that day in Kansas, I have spoken in over 400 cities and worked with over 18,000 people across hundreds of organizations. In 2005, I was hired by FranklinCovey, a leadership and performance improvement company, to deliver their core programs such as **The 7 Habits of Highly Effective People** and *Focus, Achieving Your Highest Priorities*.

My first book (a workbook, of course), **You Can, You Will, You Did, Micro Changes for Macro Transformation** (2012) was about self-empowerment and creating a life you love.

This book, **Frequency Matters,** is about harnessing that same congruent energy (personal alignment) and working collaboratively with high performing professionals to innovate, create and solve problems with greater ease.

Frequency Matters is a conversation about employee engagement as a social science, focusing on what drives the behavior of both resonate (harmonious) and dissonant (inharmonious) frequencies and the statistically implied outcomes of such clusters.

Why employee engagement?

The statistics published by Gallup Research reveal that employee engagement should be a critical focus when attempting to identify approaches for improving overall organizational performance. As a professional with years of experience, I agree.

Understanding leaders, coworkers and other employees may be as easy as understanding our own basic desires, needs and fears, as well as the clumsy ways we attempt to realize our positive intentions. It can also be as unpredictable as our unconscious triggers.

Perhaps the Gallup studies reveal that humanity as a whole is disengaging from illusions (but not organizations), and a longing for what is real and true is the new-found driver of the worldwide employee engagement pulse.

Little did I know at the time, but that city walk would turn out to be one of the most defining moments of my career. It was a choice that shifted everything to follow in a different direction, a heart-centered direction.

Most recently, when I flipped to the back of my favorite gold book while finishing the writing of this preface, I was surprised to discover that the reprint of **The Handbook to Higher Consciousness** was from 1997.

Apparently, the Ken Keyes Institute of Higher Consciousness was in the midst of reworking the company following his death in 1995.

In the Appendix of the 1975 version (1997 reprint) were the words, "This is the first reprint since Ken's passing. We are getting ready to move to North Carolina and I hope that we will be able to offer workshops by about mid-summer 1997."

Research tells me that never happened.

But it was mid-summer 1997 (July 16th to be exact) when I flew to Kansas City, was hired as a professional speaker and found this special book following a decision to trust my heart. I would go on to share Ken's effective ideas in the many workshops that followed. Perhaps we shared a resonate frequency.

Since that summer day in Kansas, I have learned that true resonance makes everything easier. When you "just know" something, it reveals an indicator of ease. When you are "turned off" by something, it is an invitation to discern. And feeling "excited" about something is a desire to engage.

ABOUT THIS BOOK

This is a book about *energy and engagement.* It is about You, Your Team and Organization.

It is about being ALIVE.

Over 20 voices came together to share their unique wisdom in various areas of expertise. Different perspectives add tremendous insight, value and wisdom.

It is organized simply, with five key sections that clearly describe a powerful and implementable formula for setting the stage in your organization for employee engagement, regardless of the size of your company or number of employees.

It is the kind of book to throw in your bag and take with you to stay inspired.

Write in the margins, action-plan your epiphanies or scribble in a notebook, but **use this tool.** Keep it alive. Engage it.

A key message in this book is the recognition of human *potential* grounded in human **need.**

This misunderstood combination has left 87% of the world's employees unengaged, so writes **Gallup.**

ABOUT YOUR FREQUENCY

The mind is a powerful **tool.** Used properly, we innovate, find solutions and create progressive advancements in the quality of life on earth. The brain is an integrated system; it has primitive as well as more advanced parts. We can get stuck in any part of our brain, good or bad. Integration is essential. The brain is also "plastic" per scientific research, meaning it can change.

The heart has the strongest **magnetism** in the human body. It has remarkable influence. Medical devices reveal the electrical impulses of the heart can influence the electrical impulses of the brain, and synchronize them. Harmonizing creates greater clarity and power.

Alignment is a recipe for success.

WHY IS A HEART-MIND CONNECTION IMPORTANT TO EMPLOYEE ENGAGEMENT?

Because *without being emotionally connected* to the work you do, studies show you will contribute and enjoy less.

Diluted contributions are expensive. Research indicates that on the topic of employee engagement, many of us on the planet are just "dialing it in".

The Voices in this book...

Chris McChesney, Greatness Igniter
Co-Author of *The 4 Disciplines of Execution, 4DX*

Shawn Herbig, Data Genius
President and Founder of IQS Research

Phil Goldfarb, Dynamic Visionary
President of legendary South Beach Hotel

Pete Boyd, Esq. General Guru
President of Paperstreet Web Design

Eric S. Czerniejewski, P.E., ENV SP, Sustainable Superhero
President, Infrastructure & Mobility Transportation Consultants, LLC

Michael Sabbag, Performance Expert
Author, Advisor, Speaker, Executive

Scott Baker, Mojo Maker
Rowan University Men's Head Soccer Coach

Jeffrey Keller, MS, MBA, Fearless Transformer
Vice President Strategic Partnerships

Bill Mackey, Festive Friend
Director of Information Systems

Cheryl Arpa, LSW, Joyful Juggler
Mom, Social Worker and Socializer

Jackie Reeves, Relationship Renovator
Senior Consultant, Communications Firm

Scott DiGerolamo, Connection Connoisseur
Vice President and Managing Director

Shahnaz Nensey, Lifestyle Luminaire
Board Certified Doctor of Natural Medicine

Roxanne Smith, Frequency Adjustor
LaHoChi Teacher/Intuitive Guide

Andi Burbank, Body Balancer
Personal Trainer and Fitness Expert

David Haskins, Master of the Microgesture
Research and Development Professional

Jill Straffi, Workaround Wizard
Make it Work Mom

Lori Riordan, HR Expert
Partner, Human Resources Consultant, Former Executive Vice President of Martha Stewart

Samantha Wheatly, Love Lady
Human Resources Executive

Maggie Macaulay, MS Ed., Elegant Educator
President and Owner of Wholehearted Parenting

FIVE KEY SECTIONS:

Section **One**:   Prepare to Win
Section **Two**:   Influence Your Landscape
Section **Three**:   Define and Refine your Culture
Section **Four**:   Engage with Authenticity
Section **Five**:   Align your Frequency

"Complexity is the enemy of execution."
- Tony Robbins

Section One

Prepare to Win

As an athlete, I often find it effective to use sports analogies to make key points when it comes to the qualities that create cohesive and successful teams.

The vision, players and practices involved in sports serve as the perfect example of the natural dynamics that can make or break a team's success. Commitment to key principles create that coveted and often immeasurable "chemistry" that wins games and championships – *or loses them when too much dissonance is present.*

To explore these ideas, I invited a collegiate athletic coach to share the principles he uses to create a cohesive, winning team.

Scott Baker's impressive track record proves that he practices and teaches the mental atmosphere necessary for success. The one quality he maintains, regardless of the team he has to work with, is that his focus is always on the player, not the game. To name just a few of Scott's achievements:

- Achieved Best Season in program's history
- Won multiple championships, including #1 national ranking
- Awarded Coach of the Year three times

Scott's principles also led to his high school and college players earning the best team grade point averages in their institutions.

Meet the Mojo Maker
...on preparing to win

"What can I do today that will distinguish me from every other coach or leader in the country for my team/program"?

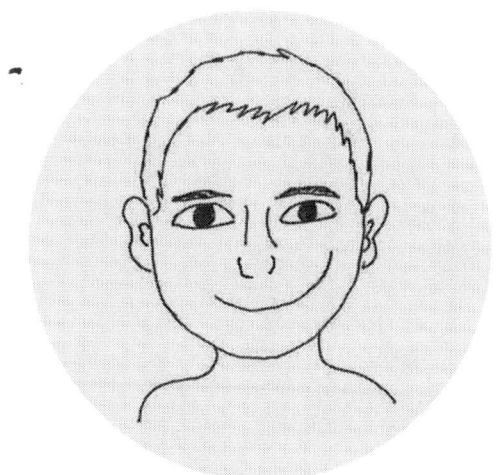

Scott Baker
Mojo Maker, Head Soccer Coach at Rowan University of New Jersey

The key word here is *distinguish*.

Whether this mantra surfaced during a one-on-one meeting, recruiting opportunity or chat with another coach, it serves as a fundamental focal point. Personally, as a leader, I gain confidence by preparing to be the best version of myself every day. This is the first step in igniting, engaging and supporting a winning team whether on the field, in the boardroom or in my community: being self-aware.

My team's vision is simple: Be the best college sports program in the country, of any sport, any division, in all areas. Living this vision daily takes extraordinary mental and physical preparation. We discuss what we call MAPS: Mental and Physical Separation. Here, the fundamental question repeats itself: "What are we doing to distinguish ourselves from every other team in the country?"

MAPS stands for *Mental And Physical Separation*. The order is important! The Mental always comes before the Physical. We look to improve from the inside out—doing this mentally before physically separates us from everyone else. Although we do not spend time comparing ourselves to other programs, we take pride in distinguishing ourselves in the way that we train and prepare all year round. As athletes, we have standards of excellence that we hold ourselves to, and these standards have led to habits and practices that set us apart from any other program in the country, as well as all sports and divisions in all areas, both in and out of the classroom.

The idea is not to compete with other teams mentally, but to strive to be better versions of ourselves *first*. Then we can completely dominate any opponent or challenge we face, which in turn creates more MAPS as we progress. We do everything with a National Championship Mindset – as people, students and athletes – in that order.

We are a cohesive team – a family! We put the team (a.k.a., the bigger picture) first at all times. We build the character of the individual first with principle-focused practices, and we celebrate personal and team success. We exercise this family mentality in our planning, decision-making and executing of visionary goals.

We win together, learn together and celebrate together. We learn to love and support everyone in our "team family". We look for the positive attributes of all of our team members and constantly demonstrate support for each other.

We keep a "dry season" (no alcohol or drugs), tuck our shirts in, use clean language, read uplifting books and quotes, refrain from talking back at officials, hold doors for others, give back to the community and keep our focus on being the best versions of ourselves as we nurture a National Championship Mindset in all that we do – on and off the field. We make excellence a habit.

This is our practice. We are committed to this practice. It is unique to our team and it gets extraordinary results. Excellence, once a habit, defines us as a program.

As a leader and coach, I practice being a good example when others are around, but I find it is most effective when no one is watching. I commit to driving my own energy and team engagement and keep my "own frequency" as high as possible. I consistently inspire greatness in myself and all those around me through mental programming and mindful preparation.

My BEST PRACTICE LIST as a coach:

- Lead with love and compassion
- Push people out of their comfort zones
- Stretch their imagination of what is possible for them and our team – and consistently expand my own expectations of what

is possible as well
- Remind them daily that it is ALL created from the inside out
- Understand that hard work gives the confidence to create miracles and achieve extraordinary results!

Our program requires that our results are created in the mind before they are demonstrated on any field as there is a mental picture before the physical in all that we do. This consistent practice creates a powerful paradigm shift that can be felt at every practice and every game. We perceive ourselves as outstanding people, students and players with great character first; then we transfer that level of performance to all that we do.

Another standard of excellence we practice is called Championship Habits. This involves true preparation and effective action planning to create the habits necessary for success. We create a training environment that is higher than the level of our opponents. We look to make practices more challenging than games. Everyone on the team is responsible for building this training environment.

We are aware of the extraordinary results that we have already created and will physically experience. It is important for me that all of my players know that love and care for them as people and players is my highest priority as a coach.

My sincere belief in each player allows them to take action with the confidence needed to achieve the vision I propose. As leaders, we must be trusted – and trust is earned with our own commitment to living the best lives we can live. Seeing players reach the heights you set out for them and witnessing them transcend their own limited beliefs because of your faith and guidance is the most rewarding experience to have a coach.

The decision and commitment to *distinguish yourself* and define and exercise your unique voice is an act of supreme courage.

By distinguishing ourselves, we tap into our true passions and tendencies. We become better acquainted with who we are, what we desire and what we value.

The playing field is the dichotomy that produces genius.

As a motivational speaker, I was required to inspire regardless of circumstance. If I did not get sleep due to a faulty itinerary, I performed. If something changed last minute, I performed. If the technology failed, the temperature hit 100 degrees or dropped below 30, I performed (once with my audience in blankets).

If I drove through a brush fire, hail storm or away from a tornado in North Dakota, I still performed. Or if we had six hotel fire drill evacuations, I simply finished where I left off, for the seventh time.

In short, no matter what, I performed. I would block mental noise from my own habitual thinking patterns and do the job. I love what I do, so it was an easy choice. That said, on the most difficult of days, I would order a brownie sundae from room service and treat myself to an overpriced in-room movie.

To consistently succeed at the task at hand, I had no choice but to commit to practices that shifted me into positivity:

1. Don't *judge* the situation as "good" or "bad;" remain detached and objective. This kept me from polluting my delivery with negative thoughts and feelings.
2. Put my *attention* on a positive outcome (what I wanted to happen).
3. Make a conscious decision to *go with the flow* (no resistance).

In hindsight, I realize that practicing such habits served as a sort of frequency maintenance. I highly recommend you try these practices for yourself.

Then came the year when I was tested beyond anything I had faced before. I had a full plate, no down time, a debilitating commute into a congested city, high-stakes keynotes and important projects alongside weighty personal challenges. In addition to this overwhelming day-to-day flurry, I experienced three significant deaths of loved ones in one year's time.

Oh yeah, and I was supposed to "look good" but would mindlessly grab comfort food unconsciously to ease my stressors. The brownie sundae treat became a habit, I regressed, and soon became mentally, emotionally, physically and spiritually exhausted. My life felt like my own self-created Hero's Journey, not unlike the final scene in **The Lord of the Rings**.

Due to my line of work, I was not ignorant of the good habits needed to support living a balanced life, and I credit many accomplishments to those practices. That said, life moves rapidly and, unlike our mobile phones, automatic optimization is not an app in the human biological system. If we don't pay attention to optimizing ourselves, our once straight posture in life can begin to bend.

It is no wonder the entire adult world has taken up coloring books.

Mindfulness, focus and emotional centering appear to be the new antidotes to society's rapid "updates." Social demands require us to upgrade **NOW.**

But upgrade to **what,** and **how?**

Imagine someone approaches you on the street and asks, "How is your frequency?" How would you answer? Would you freeze, respond with an enthusiastic "fantastic!" or stare in confusion: "What do you mean, my 'frequency'…?"

Simply stated, *frequency* is…

Your ENERGY.

Mojo.

Vibe.

Presence.

Wellbeing.

Instincts.

Feelings.

I like to think of frequency as our own source of energy and power.

We can align with it and use its influence, or we can cut it off and feel depleted. Understanding exactly **what gives us energy** and **what depletes us** is one of the most important insights we can have as we **prepare to win**.

Take Cesar Millan, better known as **The Dog Whisperer**. It is astonishing how effective he is in transforming violent dog behaviors into more productive responses through his successful training techniques.

What is so powerful about Cesar's work is that it almost looks like magic to onlookers. However, when you break it down, his effect is not magic at all – it is clarified, energetic presence.

Could we call it **his frequency**? Maybe. Perhaps it is his unique cocktail of thoughts, feelings, beliefs and practices that creates his clearly influential presence – a presence that appears to be the product of a consistently chosen mindset.

Our state of being is most powerful when we practice (then master) **complete personal congruency.** Our state of being can be called our **frequency.** This also applies to our teams, families and organizations.

You must make the decision first in your heart and commit to new behaviors to feel the ease of alignment. Then, put into practice routines that will ensure the right amount of flexibility to respond to life consistently and stay on your values-based track.

When we achieve this personal alignment, our talents, skills and abilities are maximized each day. Substantial research shows that when we are authentically inspired to engage, we offer our best selves, delight customers, sell more, work harder and perform well – ultimately garnering greater profits and outcomes.

In other words… we need to Align, Engage and Impact.

When we commit to an organization and the desire to make an impact daily, it means our **hearts and minds are into our jobs.**

Attempting to force that organic state is unproductive, regardless of the perks. You may win the mind, but not the heart. Alignment of both is required for engagement, high performance and commitment.

Could the employee engagement crisis imply something very exciting?

Perhaps we are shifting collectively beyond the security, sensation and power dynamics into a more harmonious way of operating. Never before have there been so many individually sourced enterprises like Airbnb and Uber. Individuals are fast becoming the new business model, and these collaborative models hint at the quantum shifts happening in how we live our lives globally.

Individuals are collaborating for a collective outcome.

In addition, the demands of life today require healthier lifestyles (more energy) and greater flexibility.
Do the models that thrive on valuing a work/life balance and trust win at the engagement game? Take Centric Consulting, rated

one of the Best Places to Work in 2016 by Glassdoor, an employee experience review wheelhouse. Centric's employees are mostly virtual, yet together. Within the top 10 was their Highest Rated CEO. Their culture is run with leadership commitment to making very happy and high-performing employees.

Many business books talk about a color, box, camp or style that every person falls into to better understand differences in the workplace. These insights are valuable. And although these tools can be effective in understanding personality types and the expected behaviors that follow, how those differences and behaviors *interface* and the potential (or extinguishing of potential) is a deeper conversation of what really creates high performing teams.

In short, it is important to recognize our responsibility to distinguish ourselves in order to offer our greatest value to the whole. It is just as critical to upgrade our collaborative skills beyond our historically hardwired win/lose conflict responses to better resolve challenging problems. Innovate solutions require the willingness to find them.

We should *encourage* those whose distinguishing quality is found in *courage itself*, because when one grabs the ball and runs toward collective progress, everyone wins.

Intention One: Prepare to Win

RECIPE FOR WINNING

1. 50% Alignment with passions, gifts, talents and strengths
2. 25% Mental focus
3. 25% Consistent practice of an aligned heart and mind

Section Two

Influence Your Landscape

It is deemed a best practice to properly evaluate a situation before making important changes when you are leading a team or organization. As a leader, you may choose to "first break all the rules" or take the time to learn the landscape.

It is recommended that you learn the landscape.

Learning the landscape is not just about understanding the industry or defaulting to a mentor for guidance—it about taking the time to truly understand the needs of the stakeholder, to sincerely listen with the intent to understand.

In healthcare, the landscape is industry specific; that is, there are always new systems, laws, and regulations that must be taken into consideration. It is also critical to understand the systemic impact any changes would have on internal stakeholders before engaging in streamlining processes.

But what if engagement is required by key stakeholders that are ***not your employees or team members,*** yet collaboration is just as critical? How would you approach the diagnostic phase of the best practice of analysis before execution? Additionally—and even more challenging—is how would you resolve problems when they arise?

As the boss or leader, you can at certain points of frustration "bang the gavel" to keep progress on track. As a team member influencing other stakeholders within an organization, you have multiple points of leverage to achieve outcomes:

1. Prepare and present a business case to the decision maker of the department (or organization) regarding the importance of the request and potential outcomes.

2. Establish a committee to garner transparency and set up a think tank on the problem with pre-established goals to find a solution, with a set timeline.

3. Influence pilot programs at the grassroots level to gather data and then present the data to key stakeholders.

There are many ways to have influence and solve problems within an organization if you focus on what you can impact. That said, when the landscape is, say, an entire city, you may need more insight on how to influence, innovate, and solve problems. This is the time to invite a civil engineer into the conversation.

Eric S. Czerniejewski
Sustainable Superhero, President of Infrastructure & Mobility Transportation Consultants

Meet the Sustainable Superhero

..on solving problems...

From the moment I saw the ***Discover Engineering*** video in high school, I knew I wanted to help solve society's engineering problems.

The realization that I could technically solve infrastructure challenges through engineering solutions was what drew me to be an engineer and continues to drive as my calling.

What is it like to have the mind of a problem solver?

A problem solver is required to have fundamental knowledge and understanding, the ability to apply this knowledge to practical problems and a refined and developed skill set for professional practice. Professional civil engineers are licensed in their profession and follow a code of ethics and fundamental canons. Engineers are tasked with maintaining the safety, health and welfare of the public.

This is powerful but seldom advertised in college textbooks.

Civil engineers as problem solvers have a critical responsibility to society to apply their knowledge in an ethical manner to offer exceptional solutions. I have learned in my 20 years in the industry that the magic tends to be found in the gray.

My school training led me to believe that technical knowledge and problems were almost unanimously black and white with virtually no middle ground. When I had to apply school teachings in real life, however, I realized the endless amount of subjectivity that impacts our communities on a daily basis.

The "magic" of problem solving occurs when you are given the opportunity to engage and collaborate with the community. The balancing act of deriving a technical solution based on the body of knowledge while factoring in a creative and innovative solution is subjective. In almost every infrastructure project, there is public involvement and outreach to the community and stakeholders.

My project example began back in the autumn of 2012 when Hurricane Sandy damaged State Road A1A severely. Portions of the road flooded, beach erosion occurred and a good section of the roadway washed out. New in my role as Transportation Manager for the City of Fort Lauderdale, I was faced with a list of problems that the storm had caused, such as the loss of the eastern sidewalk and valuable beach parking spaces.

Two phases of improvements were completed by 2015; first, a metal sheet pile wall was added along the edge of the beach to stabilize the road's foundation and preserve the travel lanes from further collapse. This solution could have been very black and white; to reconstruct the road as it was prior to the storm with little to no changes was an option. However, the community had faced nearly four continuous years of considerable change along this segment of road. The infrastructure disaster brought by Mother Nature turned into an opportunity for positive change. The local community became very involved. The homeowner's association and impacted residents gathered together and began collaborating on concept designs while local engineers from the State Transportation Department and other agency experts moved forward with plans. The bringing together of community ideas was eye-opening, and I was lucky to be so involved.

Rising tides and other climate change-related effects on the coastal community called for sustainable and green infrastructure solutions. Instead of simply rebuilding what the hurricane had damaged, the local community and the relevant government agency stakeholders collaborated to yield a more complete street with sustainable green infrastructure. State Road A1A was given a new neon-lit wave wall on top of the reinforced sheet pile wall, a new drainage conveyance system, higher road elevation, a 5' bike lane, new turn lanes and traffic signals, a beachfront promenade on the east side with a brick-paved shared path for bicycles and pedestrians, decorative turtle-friendly pedestrian lighting and new landscaped medians.

This process was inspiring to see. Just when everything was crashing down on them, those who were impacted the most showed the most strength. These residents had very strong feelings about what had just occurred and even stronger feelings of what should be done. There was a balance that was needed from all stakeholders.
They had an inherent desire for a sustainable, livable community.

What makes a sustainable, livable community?

This kind of community has a population with a strong sense of place and global responsibility. Engineers generally consider themselves problem solvers and are concerned with creating things that have never existed before. The same principle applies to life's challenges. Just as State Road A1A was forced to change based on the rising tides and water levels, so do humans adapt as we encounter the rise and fall of different phases of life. It wasn't until the community changed its perspective of the condition of State Road A1A that its members were able to collaborate on a solution bigger than each of their individual goals and objectives. To succeed in building the desired sustainable, livable community, the population needed to work toward self-reliance, be in harmony with nature, build a community culture, attain community control and meet individual needs.

The bigger visionary solutions needed to address much larger issues along State Road A1A. The need to make transportation infrastructure resilient to the effects of climate change was one. Furthermore, there was the realization that due to generational shifts, the way the society travels is changing. More and more studies show that the millennial generation has less desire to own vehicles, instead seeking alternative modes of transportation such as walking, biking and public transit. These two much larger social issues drove the innovative design solution for the road.

Residents who saw the road that took them back and forth from home every day get washed away had intense emotional reactions. The shift in the way the community members looked at this immediate inconvenience led to the creation of a more livable and sustainable community – one focused on everyone's interests, not just those of the individual.

Problem solving in a practical setting requires more than analytical skills alone.

Understanding and insight are necessary to define the problem and to envision the limitations of potential solutions. Being able shift perspective and see that changes to the use of the available right-of-way to address social equity issues became a much bigger decision. The favoring of automobile travel over other modes of transportation was evaluated in the final decision. Ultimately, it was decided to use the available right-of-way space for other modes of transportation; one conventional vehicle lane was set aside on the road segment for cyclists and pedestrians.

This decision to prioritize other modes of transportation will lead to a more healthy community and impact how the community travels. Creativity and innovation are required in generating a number of alternative scenarios, and analytical techniques must be applied to study the feasibility and obtain the best solution.

And what if your landscape is a home, or two homes, or a school?

A book about engagement that does not take into account *why* many of us go to work every day would fail in its entire message—the *wholeness*, power, and joy that come from personal congruency.

Whether our family is a group of friends, children, animals, neighbors, or comrades on a mission, "family" serves as the foundation of many of our lives.

Many teams can feel like second families. Coworkers can feel like family. Loved ones feel like family.

The same principles of respect, kindness, listening to others, and taking personal responsibility for our internal landscape before engaging coworkers and clients (and our children) apply.

Wisdom from the Joyful Juggler

On respect, courtesy and manners:

In my family, respect, courtesy and manners are imperative. To get respect you must give respect, regardless of different views. This goes hand-in-hand with being courteous. It's the little things like being mindful of someone else that teach the empathy so needed in today's society.

I engage our family by prioritizing quality time together. It's important for us to do things as a family like have movie nights or Friday Night Game Night. These create lasting memories of time shared and open doors for communication and trust. For example, baking with my girls is one of their favorite activities. This simple act of engagement goes a long way. It's about sharing an experience and learning to work together. It's team building.

I encourage and teach my children to view the world as their playground and to reach for their dreams. I encourage them to see beyond limitations.

Cheryl Arpa
Joyful Juggler, Mom, Social Worker and Socializer

Make it Work with the Workaround Wizard

On blending families:

1. Recognize the difference between what you can change and what you cannot. For example, you may not be able to diagnose a disease or make a child's disability disappear, but you can look for the best ways to help the situation. You cannot remove every obstacle from your life's path, but you can build roads or even take an airplane to get around or over that hurdle.

2. Prioritize. You can't often get 100% of everything you want out of life, at least not all at once. Figure out what is most important to you. Would you rather have new furniture or take a vacation overseas? Would your child rather have new clothes or use some hand-me-downs and take music lessons instead? Would you rather live in the city close to your work, or farther away but closer to a family/friend support network?

3. Get support. Be it family, friends, fellow church members or other people in a similar situation as yours (even an online support group!), use your support system. Read books and learn as much as you can about an obstacle, because when it comes to engagement, knowledge is power.

4. SAY THANK YOU. No matter how unbearable your life may seem at a given moment, show gratitude. Understand that others may also be fighting battles that are different, but just as powerful as yours. When you show sincere gratitude, people almost always go out of their way to lessen your burden.

Finally, keep in mind that life often has a funny way of turning what seems to be the worst situation in the short term into the best situation in the long term. Have faith!

Jill Straffi
Workaround Wizard, Make it Work Mom

The Elegant Educator

On engaging children:

Kahlil Gibran wrote, "Your children are not your children. They are the sons and daughters of Life's longing for itself." Gibran's inspiring words may ring true literally when you find your frequency at odds with your child's. In such times, your child may seem like a mystery or a stranger, not the child you thought you knew. How do you then re-engage?

First of all, slow down and get curious about what is happening with both your child and with you. Remind yourself that he is having a harder time than you are. His purpose is not to frustrate you. Take your focus off any agenda or outcome and simply get curious. From that place of curiosity, you can engage more smoothly.

Second, feel your emotions and be aware of what your body is telling you. If you are driving home from work totally consumed with a project that is not going well, take the time to feel and relax your body before you walk in the door. Your increased awareness and balanced energy will invite your children into your space rather than you jumping into theirs. Your feelings are powerful guides meant to be honored. We get into trouble in relationships when we believe we must express everything! Feel your emotions first, get curious, and then engage. How you model your energy is the most powerful teacher for your child as he learns to manage his own.

Maggie Macaulay
Elegant Educator, President and Owner of Wholehearted Parenting

Intention Two: Influence Your Landscape

RECIPE FOR A LANDSCAPE

1. 60% Passionate alignment with the landscape (industry, lifestyle, work)
2. 20% Learn how to become an effective contributor within the landscape
3. 20% Maintain a learning mindset and adapt skillfully

Section

Define and Refine your Culture

"Connect the dots between individual roles and the goals of the organization. When people see that connection, they get a lot of energy out of work. They feel the importance, dignity and meaning in their job."
Ken Blanchard

Great leadership & buy-ins create high engagement outcomes

An employee's perspective

"Kristin, you are promoted to Director of Service Excellence. Your job is to raise patient satisfaction scores for the hospital. You will oversee the Patient Relations department of 15 and report to me. Here is your budget, team and new salary – oh, and **the sky is the limit.**"

This was what my mentor said to me in the administrative building of a children's hospital following my forgoing a vacation in the hope of a promotion very early in my career.

After traveling as a professional speaker for two solid years, I was tired and craving the comfort of being part of an organization and having that sense of community. In reality, the sky **was not** the limit per his words, but his message was clear: I believe in you, I will support you and I will not limit your talent.

Deal.

To rally a 2,300-employee operation toward technical, behavioral and statistically measured outcomes demanded an unconventional approach. Instead of the usual long meetings, memos and training calendars posted in waiting areas, we decided to drive engagement by personally involving everyone before the launch.

We created flyers and training programs as "teasers" for what was to come. We walked from unit to unit, handing out materials that hinted at our event with slogans like "Don't Miss! Service Excellence Kick-off." Walking the floor, talking to employees and meeting with every department head to access their needs before designing the plan forward laid the groundwork for a fully engaged hospital.

We implemented many practices that resulted in a direct increase in our patient satisfaction scores. The changes included: redesigning the department, giving market raises, training leaders and staff, hanging bulletin boards in every department to visibly track progress, and implementing software to provide real-time data for leaders to make prompt changes.

The sessions we led were not your typical mandatory trainings; in fact, they were not mandatory at all. And yet, every class was filled to standing room only. Employees and leaders alike were excited and involved in the new Service Excellence vision. Because we involved everyone in the planning stages of the initiative, everyone was already engaged when we rolled it out.

Engagement is about interaction. By involving the staff in our initial concepts, we gave them a stake in the outcome of the program. To force engagement is not engagement; buy-in comes from giving employees the chance to make an informed choice.

My senior leader encouraged these innovative approaches that ultimately improved patient satisfaction scores, made for clearer discharge instructions and brought about a seamless collection process.

LEADERSHIP IS THAT IMPORTANT.

Committed and experienced leaders offer necessary direction in industries like healthcare where critical policies and standards are essential and employees are held accountable. This transparency allows the leader to best position creative employees for success without going beyond the boundaries of safety and quality.

"When trying to improve engagement, over 90% of the time, answers can be found by looking at the leadership team, the relationships within the team or the relationships between the team members and the department or company."

Shawn Herbig
Data Genius
President and Founder of IQS Research

Another example of great leadership is in those who create a positive culture themselves.

Creating a resonant culture

How cool people start businesses and become great leaders.

Pete Boyd attributes his tenacity and methods to his roots. "My parents raised me to have the willpower to overcome anything. When you combine willpower and passion for what you do, difficulties are easier," says Boyd. "Running a business is mostly being a jack-of-all trades, and being a master of most of them. It is also good to have a niche." If you have passion, a plan and time to invest, you can start a business at any age.

"Starting, running and succeeding in business is no easy task considering 44% of start-ups fail within the first 3 years and a whopping 60% fail at the six-year mark. PaperStreet Web Design has thrived for well over a 15 years now. They have won more than 50 awards, designed over 1,000 websites and helped clients all across the world."

What does Paperstreet do to be Paperstreet? I asked the General Guru himself…

Pete Boyd
General Guru, President of Paperstreet Web Design

Our Vision

A plan always starts with a vision. What do you want to accomplish? We at Paperstreet establish our personal and professional vision on a yearly basis. Business and family tend to change annually, so it is great to update frequently. Yes, we have an overall vision long-term, but make slight revisions along the way. Typically around the holidays we start to review the year. We look at analytics, what went wrong, what went right, what do we want to do the next year and the next five years.

The key to life, work, teams and projects is balance. Working too hard in one area will impact other areas negatively. If you are spending too much time at work, your personal life will suffer (family, friends, yourself). If you spend too much time on your personal life, your professional life may begin to slip.

Our vision for the business is to provide a responsive team that can assist law firms with web design, internet marketing and content. Our vision for the family is to simply be there – this means not working 50- or 60-hour work weeks. When you only have to work 35 to 40 hours, this frees up a lot of time for family and friends, which makes for an overall better lifestyle.

At Paperstreet, we set up and strive for a 35-hour work week. Do we work 40-hour weeks? Sure. There are times when we need to work hard to finalize projects. However, by setting the expectation to work 35 hours, we're still only at a standard company's work week even if we overstay 5 hours.

Our expectations are set up so that work is not everything in life. This also means that when we are at work, we are 100% working. There is little time to waste with Facetime or inefficient meetings. The team must focus, given that we are trying to hit a lower overall hour count per week. Overall, we find it a good motivator to get things done.

Hiring Talent

Now that we know our vision, we identify what it takes to accomplish our goals. Most often this requires talent. We hire talent through a standard process that works well.

First, we outline exactly what we want for the position. Next, we think of our ideal candidate and write a personal ad geared towards attracting that person. Are they young and interested in video games? Then we hype the fact that we play a lot of games at work during our lunch hour. Is the candidate more experienced and has a family? Then we state that we have a flexible work environment, a 35-hour work week and the option to work remote. Every candidate is different and you need to write your ad for the specific person you want.

We of course post online ads, but also ask internally if anyone knows of a friend. A lot of our best hires are from referrals. For the hiring, we typically get 50 resumes in for every person we hire. We narrow that down to a list of 5 to 10 people whom we want to interview, and then we conduct 15-minute interviews on the phone and secondary interviews for more detail.

There are two key parts to our interviewing process. First is no mistakes. We request candidates to follow specific directions in the form of a pass/fail test. We are a detailed worked environment and we want to minimize mistakes as much as possible. If a candidate cannot follow the instructions on the application or interview, then they probably will not fit with our company.

Second, we always do live work projects. These are paid assignments, but they tell us whether the candidate can deliver on time, on budget and with great quality. It is absolutely necessary to have a working relationship before we hire. It helps both our company and the candidate to see if they want and can do the job.

It is very important to us that we hire no drama queens (or kings). People who bring in personal issues, professional issues, or are just not fun to be around during work are simply not hired. Even if they are really talented, if they do not make work fun they will not fit with our culture. We are always short on hours in the day, so we do not have time to deal with people who bring in drama. We want reliability in our team so that we can focus on the tasks at hand.

Overall, we keep our team happy by making sure everyone is working on a worthwhile project where they can personally make an impact. Being stuck on a project that has no purpose or feels stagnant is never fun. Being a team member with little impact on the company is also deflating. So, we make sure that everyone enjoys what they are doing and understands why it is important.

We also are fairly autonomous at our jobs. Each team is run by a director. Goals are set at director meetings, but each director is individually responsible for hitting the goals. We don't like to micromanage unless we see that something simply is not working. That same autonomy is passed down to our teams, where each teammate is responsible for an entire project, whether it be design, development, content or marketing.

Finally, we provide a dependable environment. We have grown slowly over 15 years, hiring a few people per year. We do not want to ever have to lay off individuals because management took a big gamble and failed. We allow remote work, have our 35-hour work week, and our pay is even with other companies (so you end up working less and making the same).

When you combine offering worthwhile projects, the ability to make an impact, personal autonomy and a dependable work environment, you can make any team happy.

Now there are times when you need to make tough decisions. Often, this comes when you need to fire someone. However, you will find that teams don't want to work with people who suck. To be blunt, they want to work with people they like and who are competent. If you have people who need to be fired, then get rid of them instantly. Your team will actually thank you and your productivity will increase. Firing is never a fun day, but it can improve teams in the long term.

On the flip-side is hiring. We love to hire. However, you should only hire when you absolutely need the position. Hire when you have clear goals for the position and quantifiable deliverables. For example, if we are hiring a content writer, we may want them to produce 5 pages a day of text for our website or be able to edit 25 pages of text. If we are hiring a designer, we may want them to be able to produce one new home page concept a day. Have specific deliverables so you can know when an employee can meet those goals. If you hire without goals, then you are setting the position up to not improve, or at worst, to fail.

Once you have hired, you need to motivate your team. We first look for candidates who are internally motivated. Our entire team wants to be the best at their given craft. However, even the best need some help along the way so they do not get bored.

We try to help by figuring out what each person is motivated by. Some are motivated by money – okay, set up bonuses. Others are motivated by time off – so give them more time off. Others are motivated by being left alone – give them more autonomy and demand fewer reports and meetings.

Long term, we develop talent by attending the usual conferences and reading . . . a lot. Almost every team member reads on their own time to improve their skill sets.

Engagement

We engage the team on six levels: we have cool meetings, fun events, a fun environment, we set goals, focus on the practical and just win.

1. **Cool Meetings.** Our entire team has been running "cool" meetings for 10 years now – we meet once a week to go over anything cool. The team sends in links to a set email address (cool@****) to projects they are proud of, interesting websites or anything creative. This works to get everyone involved on a weekly basis.

2. **Fun Events.** Trampolining, skeet shooting, kayaking, paddle boarding, hockey games, paint ball, Halloween contests, holiday parties, free lunches, happy hours, you name it. We are even gearing up for a bubble soccer event. Keeping it mixed up means that everyone has something to look forward to.

3. **Create a Fun Environment.** We painted a chalkboard in our office and allowed everyone to post their favorite quotes. It is great to see what inspires everyone.

4. **Set Goals.** Everyone wants to do great work, but that work must have a purpose. Set team goals that are tied to your core business and track those goals. This will lead to more engagement from your team as they reach their goals, more feedback and more interactions.

5. **Focus on the Practical.** For a distributed team, you need to communicate effectively. Without this, everything fails. We use Slack for quick chats, Google Docs for documents and our own dashboard to track time, projects, clients and goals.

6. **Just Win.** Winning solves everything and motivates everyone. Set up tasks so that each person can win personally and the team can win overall. This can include awards for design, proposals for new business, sales, marketing goals for the team, solving a tech issue or anything that advances the business. Just win.

Leadership

Leaders lead by example. They should always be available. They should be ready to step in at any time and do anything on the team. They should also work the same hours as their teams. This helps everyone know that they are not alone and keeps jealousy away. The worst thing a leader can do is announce an emergency project and then go home for the day.

I have personally answered the phone on Christmas to assist clients with their websites. We once pulled an all-nighter to move over 200 websites to a new server in under four hours. The team stayed together until the project was done. I have even given out my personal mobile number to all 500 clients and let them know they could call at any time for any reason.

Work/Life Balance

Putting in fewer hours allows us to have a real work/life balance. We strive for a 35-hour work week, which allows our team to actually be at home for family and friends.

We do have set goals per month, but they are based on realistic hours. We are also flexible when it comes to those goals. If you miss a monthly goal, simply make it up the next month.

We love goals. We love autonomy. We love charts and checklists to make sure everything is on track. With a simple, quantifiable goal, everyone can see that they are going to be on track. If someone isn't on track, we don't yell or scream. Rather, we figure out why that person didn't hit the goals. The key is to make sure you check on progress regularly, not just the week before the goal's due date.

For instance, we want to have 100 billable hours each month per employee on the support team. They know this is the goal. They can break it down easily in that with 20 working business days per month (on average), they need to hit five billable hours per day. So they have a daily count to hit, a weekly goal and a monthly goal. With that knowledge, they can easily plan out the week and tasks. This is all backed up in a time tracking and project management tool that can be queried at any time to kick out the numbers needed. So the goal is set, the individual is on their own to work toward the goal and we have a checklist or chart to track progress.

The Paperstreet Web Design Team

Shawn Herbig
Data Genius, President and Founder of IQS Research

"You have to love your employees like they are your kids. When this was a $10 million company I knew everyone by name, but I can't do that now."

Those were some of the first words shared during my conversation with Charles Price, President of Charah. Charles and his team grew the company from $10 million in revenue to over $250 million and increased their employee count eight-fold during a ten-year period. And they aren't done yet.

This type of growth takes a lot of effort. Sixty- and seventy-hour work weeks are common.

> "There were many times something would go wrong at a client site and I would put the management team on a plane so we could meet

with the client that day or first thing the next morning."

When your job is to grow the company, meet the needs of the client and the needs of government regulators, there aren't a lot of hours left in the day to focus on employee development. Further, when your team is expected to work just as hard as you are, there is precious little time available for them to grow. And to make things more difficult, this challenge doesn't stand still. As the company continues to grow, the pressure to perform increases, which further limits the time available to grow the team.

Challenging? Yes!

But, successful leaders don't have the luxury of self-pity.

There will always be time constraints, even when you have invested time to accomplish our long-term goals. You still need to invest in people as individuals and as teams. Leaders have a responsibility to keep their people headed in the right direction, engaged, motivated and connected, all while meeting the day-to-day needs of the business.

Charah relies on four people strategies for growth:

1. Hire people who are wired the right way.
2. Sincerely listen to your people.
3. Measure effectively and course-correct as necessary.
4. Reward hard work.

People who are wired in The Charah Way understand that long hours are the norm. They understand that can mean missed meals, changing plans and nights on the road. Charah has recognized that this is part of how the company conducts business, so instead of trying to mitigate these factors, the team acknowledges and is transparent with new employees about expectations. Instead of focusing on work/life balance (an admirable goal, to be sure), they instead focus on work hard/play hard. Transparency ensures that people understand the demands and that there are no surprises.

Listening to people is easier when the organization is small and the leadership team knows everyone by name. As the organization grows, that dynamic changes. Fast growth in the number of employees also generates unique issues – like when suddenly half the employee base has worked at the company for less than three years. When this happens, tenured employees often have a hard time understanding their roles. Walking down the hallway and not knowing the names of one's peers can be unsettling, but is very common.

Charah has been a client of IQS Research since 2009 when we implemented a company-wide tool to listen to employees, measure their engagement and identify opportunities to improve. The company's leaders maximize the limited time they have to get the greatest return on employee experience.

> "If we think about the business like a ship, then effective employee feedback is the rudder. You have to know which way the rudder is facing or the ship will never get you where you want to go."

In the end it isn't enough just to listen to your employees; there has to be a commitment to improve. That commitment has to be practiced throughout the organization. By combining its people metrics, company metrics and client metrics, Charah was able to make process adjustments and be intentional with its efforts.

This practice has taken effect throughout the company. Employees have internalized an entrepreneurial spirit and take responsibility for the organization's success by holding each other accountable for performance. Since a lot is expected of everyone, there is a standard that anyone not pulling their own weight will be called out.

As Charah grows, the company's engagement scores continue to rise. The only time scores declined was when company growth slowed. Charah's people are wired for growth and are most engaged when that is happening.

As success is generated, people should expect to be rewarded. Perhaps it makes sense to expand the saying to "work hard, play hard, pay well." This is also a Charah belief that helps attract and retain their best people.

> "There is a pot of gold at the end and we need to try to distribute that out."

People need to know that they will be rewarded for their commitment and long hours. That can come in many forms for an organization, and we have seen organizations implement very creative strategies for flexibility, vacations, company-paid trips and financial incentives like bonuses and raises. The combination can be unique to each organization as long as everyone feels that their hard work is appreciated.

A FEW UNIVERSAL TRUTHS

- Leadership is critical to individual performance and team performance.

- Everyone walks in with skills, but you have to earn credibility.

- People want good leaders. When bad leadership leaves the company, the employees are typically pleased.

- Everyone has to earn their keep.

- Employee feedback is about humility.

- It takes a while to develop trust and confidence in your people, but once you do, you have to let them go and do their jobs. You can't be the crutch that holds them back.

A great leader consistently <u>creates the space</u> that inspires quality contributions.

A great contributor <u>aligns with a culture that resonates, prepares to win and makes an impact.</u>

Other times, we just need to LISTEN UP!

Over years of working with organizations, we have observed thousands of factors that support or inhibit engagement. The following scenarios are some of the more common ways we have seen engagement – or disengagement – come to life within a company. Each one is important to help you, as a leader, know where you are starting and what situation you have so that you know where to begin.

- ***Don't eat your young.*** Employees who have been around the longest are often not accepting of new employees and can be so harsh that the new employees eventually quit. The department scores average out to be good, but a closer look reveals that some people love their experience while others hate it.

- ***Engagement: It is important to keep an eye on the unique sentiments brewing in your team.***

- ***Accommodating management isn't leadership.*** Many leaders think that they need to be easy and friendly with their employees, but that isn't always the answer. Employees look for leadership and expect you to lead. While a leader isn't a dictator, someone will have to make the final decision – most employees want to be involved in that decision, but not necessarily as the person who makes it. If a leader lacks the will to hold employees accountable, some people will take advantage of that and may even go around the leader.

- ***Engagement: Transparency, trust, and integrity are essential for all teams. Members may disagree with each other, but it is critical to keep all perceptions, concerns, ideas, and even disagreements on and above the table.***

- ***Managers without self-awareness are often surprised by results.*** They hear "everything is fine!" and then fail to understand why their department scores are so low. Results in these cases often paint a picture of a directive leader with only one form of communication, thereby missing out on connections with the team and opportunities to improve.

- ***Tell me who it is and I will fire them.*** Working for your company should be treated as a privilege. At the same time, managers cannot punish people for expressing their opinions, even when those opinions don't make us feel good. Leadership development is important, especially when it comes to self-awareness.

- ***Engagement: The strongest and most influential leaders*** *are the most honest, transparent, and forthright. They speak clearly and honestly with all team members about issues and concerns and are open about their own strengths and weaknesses. The strong leader is there to lead, be an example, and be constantly focused on how one's presence impacts the whole, removing barriers, streamlining processes, and helping the team collaborate well together to achieve common goals. She does not simply seek to advance the status of the individual leader because she knows that engagement would never follow from this behavior.*

- *New leadership knows everything.* When a new team takes over an organization, it is easy to act like they are the only ones who know the "right way" to do things. Everyone who isn't part of the new guard is relegated to tier-2 status.

- *Engagement: Identify what has worked in the past and be open to different perspectives when gathering information.*

- *The team doesn't want a leader.* A team unites around a common enemy – the manager. When this happens, team scores are often unusually high but leadership scores are low. This shows that even good managers can struggle to create a cohesive unit.

- *Engagement: Always pay attention to the climate of the team to proactively correct their course when necessary.*

Direct feedback is the key to improvement. Unless we are open and willing to talk honestly, we run the risk of wasting time in the midst of trying to solve costly problems. That said, we can be both direct *and* kind.

If you want to create team resonance, begin with establishing quality relationships with the people you work with each day. These relationships do not flourish from a single conversation, but rather come from continuous interaction, feedback loops, and tackling challenges together.

The Relationship Renovator
On engagement:

1. Build it – the relationship, that is – and they will come. Get to know your team and allow them to get to know you to establish an environment of trust.

2. Engage the "disengaged" with new opportunities to recharge and recommit. Motivation is different for different people.

3. Give and receive the gift of feedback.

Jackie Reeves
Relationship Renovator, Senior Consultant, Communications Firm

The Fearless Transformer
On walking the walk:

1. Be genuinely interested in what staff want to develop in their lives, not just what they can do better for you.

2. Openly encourage staff to bring their problems to you, especially personal ones. Caring about what bothers them most helps them to care about what bothers you most.

3. Don't just share details . . . explain yourself. Most people can handle the WHAT and HOW if you tell them WHY.

4. Engagement is a daily thing, not an annual review thing. It takes organization and effort to do it and still get everything else done.

5. High performance and engagement go hand-in-hand. Engagement for the sake of engagement is a waste of time, energy and resources. Gear every conversation toward improving staff performance in some way.

Jeffrey Keller
Fearless Transformer, Vice President Strategic Partnerships

Tidbits from the Connection Connoisseur

On making connections:

1. Tell your story, stories connect us
2. Care about your clients and what they need
3. Be honest, have the critical conversations
4. Have passion and enthusiasm for what you do

Scott DiGerolamo
Executive

Wisdom from the Performance Expert

On best practices:

Hire for fit.
If the people you hire are committed to the purpose, mission, vision and values of the organization, you will have full engagement.

Meet needs.
Organizations and people both have needs. It is the intersection of those needs where you create the opportunity for the employee to win by leveraging her/his strengths and the organization to win by gaining exemplary performance.

Focus on people.
The only way to execute strategy is through highly capable and productive people. Do everything you can to enable this.

Develop first, manage last.
If you are constantly helping people grow in their careers and achieve higher levels of performance, the need to manage them is rare.
Your purpose, mission, vision and values should guide decisions. This makes them real and reinforces their importance to the people who joined because of who the organization *is* rather than what it ***does***.

Michael Sabbag
Performance Expert,
Author of *Developing Exemplary Performance One Person at a Time*

Master of the Microgesture

On kindness and fun:

Tolerance.
People will make mistakes. We all do. Be understanding of their shortcomings and you'll build trust. Snub them or shoot them down and you'll lose them. Innovative research work requires experimentation, and this includes feeling safe to express ideas, even if they seem completely off-the-wall.

Humor, humor and more humor.
Nothing is more of a buzzkill to a meeting or an engagement than a serious tone that brings a cloud over the room. Humor lightens and allows me to connect with people on a human level. Think of the times when you bonded with someone most; you probably were laughing out loud. Humor is especially great for building instant rapport with a stranger, and

Empathy.
Everyone has a day where they are depressed, scared, not feeling confident or just having generally tough time. It's on those days that I offer my ear and hear people out generously. I know I need that when I'm in a funk. Lots of times, life gets us bunched up in knots and we just need someone to vent to. One moment of helping someone ground themselves in a crisis might save them and those around them from being pulled into unnecessary, escalating drama.

David Haskins
Master of the Microgesture,
Research and Development Professional

Reflections from the HR Expert

On putting the "Human" back in Human Resources:

There is only way to ensure the success of HR – put the "human" back into Human Resources.

The success of any performance review, termination or employee retention goal depends on what relating took place. HR are constantly in the position of relating to others, and they must do it well.

Everyone knows a leader has to communicate well, possess the knowledge to lead and be a team player, but none of that matters if the leader cannot inspire others. The primary way the leader conveys their passion is by working alongside ALL employees.

HR leaders must do the same. Employees are not just clients; HR begins a fragile, vulnerable relationship with every employee, and the manner in which this relationship is approached determines its ultimate success.

That said, nothing surpasses hard work. Experience and knowledge cannot be achieved without time invested. The most successful people have a story of how hard they worked before they reached success. They were willing to do any job and work as many hours as was needed to get the job done. It speaks to their discipline and work ethic. Further, an HR leader's work ethic is critical to setting the tone of the department. A clock puncher or a rigid rule follower is not going to create an environment within the company where employees feel welcome, safe or desired.

Employees need to know that if they come to HR, they can trust us and feel safe. Trust is critical to all relationships, work or personal, and if an employee can't trust you, then the relationship can't even start.

Lori Riordan
HR Expert, Former Executive Vice President of Human Resources for Martha Stewart

Intention Three: Define and Refine your Culture

RECIPE FOR CULTURE

1. 90% Leadership-driven and supported
2. 5% Rock star performers set the bar
3. 5% Train and support the rock stars to be the next leaders

Section **Four**

Engage with Authenticity

I joined the FranklinCovey team back in 2005 as a consultant on core programs. I'd had a FranklinCovey planner ever since I could remember and "resonated" with the company's vision, content and practices.

During that time, I recall attending a workshop in Alpharetta, Georgia where the energetic Chris McChesney gave a dynamite speech. Within five minutes of being in a room with Chris, I realized I did not need another sip of coffee – his energy alone triggered my instant engagement.

One does not forget such talent. He was authentic, engaging and a powerful communicator.

Years later, I was hired and tasked with taking over the performance, training and quality initiatives for an organization slated to face some exciting internal changes. I trusted in the quality of the FranklinCovey content and decided to utilize a recipe of materials I was confident would help me achieve what appeared to be a lofty goal.

1. Maintain successful engagement efforts through the internal changes.
2. Engage talented executives to synergize performance improvement.
3. Maintain or improve employee engagement via leadership development.

The team was service-focused, high-performing and often celebrated.

Where to start?

Engagement: You have to understand it to fix it.

There has been a lot of talk about employee engagement in the last few years. We need to be careful that when we refer to engagement, we are using tools that measure *employee* engagement. To do so, we must know what we mean by engagement and how it comes to life on a team.

People often say that engagement is more than a measurement – it is something that needs to be done every day. I completely agree! In addition, a reliable assessment of your team's engagement will tell you precisely where you stand and how you can improve.

There are many different ways to define engagement, but I like to use a basic definition based on output which says that an engaged [employee, associate, customer, volunteer, audience member] person will give discretionary effort to go above and beyond or to overcome an obstacle. They do it because their needs are aligned with their department, their boss, their work or their company. They have achieved a harmonious frequency and it shows in their energy, enthusiasm and attentiveness.

Yes, it is true that companies with engaged employees will perform better. This is obvious, but the path to achieve engagement has some built-in stepping stones.

First, a person must be satisfied with their experience. Satisfaction is often confused with engagement, but being satisfied is only one part of being engaged.

Second, the person begins to identify with the organization. This is an important step where the person begins to adopt and internalize the organization's characteristics.

Third, they begin to show commitment to the organization. A committed employee will turn down competitive job offers and often won't even take a call from a headhunter.

Fourth, the employee begins to exhibit increased performance. This is often considered the Holy Grail of employee engagement – this is the last phase of engagement.

To measure engagement, we have to be sure we have an accurate measure of satisfaction, identity, commitment and performance. In the end, you have to know how engaged your team is or what holds back their engagement; find out what is messing with their frequency and what can be done to increase engagement and get their frequency back in line.

As an employee working within a system, were it not for the expertise of IQS Research, the challenge of identifying where to focus, what to invest in and what to measure (aligned with our top organizational goals) would have been too difficult.

When you are looking at 50 items that pull your attention, time and resources, it is critical to seek proper and skilled direction *before* investing in efforts. This arms you with a solid and measurable plan to best focus your energy on a few key items that will make the biggest difference in achieving your top organizational goals.

Verdict: measure, seek expertise and invest in behavior-based training.

At the close of this implementation chapter was an amazing talk by my former colleague and co-author of **The 4 Disciplines of Execution (4DX)**. It included outstanding feedback from the 40 leaders and executives now holding the baton.

I credit the president of the organization at the time for setting the organizational tone for the many high-performing individuals, as well as important performance standards and key goals (engagement being a top priority). And of course, the FranklinCovey content that served as the best toolkit to purchase for this exciting leadership mission must also be recognized.

In the history of my career, this south beach resort was one of the best examples of a harmonious, engaged and consistently excellent organization that I ever witnessed. It was also the most diverse. The leader was visionary, dynamic, compassionate and engaged. Never underestimate the power of one leader's frequency.

Lead with passion, measure with precision.

Shawn Herbig
Data Genius, President and Founder of IQS Research

Insights from the Data Genius

When I started my career, I was a very driven young person with big ideas (or so I thought), strong opinions, boundless energy and an inherent lack of ability to censor my words. This last characteristic landed my foot in my mouth more times that I care to count.

One of those times was when I was working on the Ford Explorer engineering team (the PVT). I was working on a project and needed some information from a co-worker. Unfortunately, this co-worker and I didn't naturally hit it off. He was a great guy, we were just different and that came out when we had to work together.

My project was getting behind and my boss was becoming impatient with me. One morning during the team meeting, my boss put me on the spot (again) and asked me – rather heatedly – when I was going to be done. I answered, "When my jerk co-worker finally gives me the information I've have been requesting!"

Two things to note here: I didn't actually see the word "jerk", and the guy was sitting right behind me.

Definitely not a moment I was proud of, but it happened. Yes, I had made numerous requests for the information. Yes, this person was being willfully negligent in withholding the information and yes, I was at my boiling point. None of that justified my words.

After the meeting, I had to sit across the desk from my (very angry) boss, next to my (very offended) co-worker. I felt like I was in the principal's office in school. Suffice it to say, I promptly received the information I needed and I apologized.

Sitting at my desk about an hour later, I felt like a complete fool. I knew I had been out of line. About that time, my friend Dave came up and asked if we could talk in private. I had always had a lot of respect for Dave; he was one of the smartest people I have ever met. Prior to working together, I think he designed a missile system . . . just a super smart guy.

Dave and I walked over to the copier. He looked me right in the eyes and said, "You know you screwed up, right?" He had a slight smile on his face but he was very serious. In the tone of a big brother, he put his hand on my shoulder and calmly explained to me what I was already thinking. He told me that I had every right to be frustrated but had done damage to my reputation with my response. He then reminded me that to build my career I needed to do things differently and gave me several steps to take and changes to make. And he was right.

What I still appreciate about that talk is that Dave approached me at a difficult time with a difficult conversation, but he did it in a way that was without judgement and completely with my best interest in mind. It didn't feel good, but it was exactly the conversation I needed.

As my career has progressed, I have come to appreciate how important it is for someone to be willing to have difficult, honest, judgement-free conversations with another person. I have also found that most people want honesty as long as they trust the motives of the person delivering the message.

So, when I am working with a young (or young at heart) leader who has big ideas, boundless energy and an engagement problem they are trying to solve, I look at that person (with a slight smile and total seriousness) and have a conversation with their best interest at heart. Oftentimes that is the only tool that can authentically move a person forward.

FEEDBACK AND TRUST

One fine day I, Kristin, found myself in the Emergency Room of a fairly prestigious hospital with a deep cut in my hand. I was bleeding everywhere. It had all started with a cookie.

In Florida, the air is moist and things tend to get soggy, so everything gets put in the refrigerator, including cookies. After a long day, I looked to the refrigerator for a treat.

Upon pulling out the dish, my desired cookie appeared frozen to the plate. Stuck solid. I grabbed a metal spatula to pry the cookie off the plate. It did not work.

I then angled the spatula in an attempt to flick the cookie into the air, off the plate and into my hungry mouth. No such luck. So, I pushed **really** hard and the spatula slipped over the stubborn cookie – right *into* my hand.

I raced to the ER, driving while blood soaked through my homemade towel-bandage, and thought, "All this over a cookie…"

I must have been quite the sight because I was taken to the back immediately. A very young man looked at my injury.

He appeared more nervous than I was; I could feel his hands shaking as he evaluated my wound. Once he geared up with his tools, he began cleaning and stitching **but was still shaking**. He was shaking so badly that at one point I had to tell him to breathe. "It's fine, you can do this," I said.

He stitched each knot so slowly and nervously, I even cheered him on.

Across the way, a man must have overheard my cheering because he strolled inconspicuously past to peek at the wound.

He then ever so quietly leaned in and gently addressed us in a whisper, "You need to reverse the knots to secure them or they will fall out."

Um.

He then quietly disclosed that he was an oral surgeon visiting his mother (she was resting nearby). She waved.

The young doctor looked horrified and immediately agreed. "Oh yes, so sorry, so sorry!" and rushed to redo all the already-stitched knots in my hand.

Again, I thought, "Over a cookie..."

As he redid his work one stitch at a time, I desperately tried not to pass out.

When the job was finally done, the attending physician came by to check the work and asked before discharging me, "How did he do?"

"He did a fine job as I am all repaired, it looks clean and I am ready to go now please," I said.

The attendant inspected the stitching, said "Excellent work!" to the young doctor and walked away.

The young doctor looked like the weight of the world had lifted. He jumped to hug me, saying "Thank you so much, thank you, thank you! This is my first day out of medical school and you were my first patient."

Years later I barely have a scar – he **was** good, just nervous.

Clearly this young doctor was well trained, otherwise he would not have been hired at this highly respected hospital. He was also very skilled after some mentoring. Imagine how the scene would have gone without patience, compassion and humility?

I like to imagine that he went on to save many lives with more confidence then he had on his first day of work.

MENTORING

I credit the success of my own career to mentors. Mentors that I respected, trusted and have built truly enriching relationships with over the many years.

The ability to reach out to others you trust for advice (and offer it), or sometimes simply laugh at ironic situations is what creates those lifelong and rewarding connections. Mentoring is even more critical in a high-intensity environment where employees are required to make fast, accurate decisions – or in my case, stitch a hand.

Verdict: If you are a leader, mentor others. Mentor daily. Mentor often.

Great mentors nurture great teams; this can be the difference between a harmonious team and a one that is unraveling.

THE DIFFERENCE BETWEEN HARMONIOUS AND INHARMOUS FREQUENCIES

Problems, conflicts and challenges are a part of life.

Excellent communication is required during times of conflict to avoid triggering a pre-existing neuropathway, most often showing its presence as *a reaction.*

Communication with more harmonious frequencies may be sloppier in form, yet surprisingly more effective on the level of understanding due to harmonious frequencies. For example, have you ever found that you relate better to someone who speaks an entirely different language or comes from a completely different culture than someone from your hometown?

That is frequency resonance.

Another example of this can be witnessed in Tony Robbins' Netflix Documentary, *I am Not Your Guru*. The audience members come from all over the world, speak multiple languages and have vastly different backgrounds. However, what drove them to choose a Tony Robbins' program was rooted in frequency.

The most powerful driver among this audience was their ***desire for a life change***. That was the common ground. That energy, desire and hope trumped any differences, establishing a harmonious frequency.

A shared goal can instantly harmonize frequencies.

The article "The Worldwide Employee Engagement Crisis" published in ***Gallup*** states that the world has an employee engagement crisis, with serious and potentially lasting repercussions for the global economy. The article expands on a distinctive quality of how organizations approach employee engagement:

> *Creating a culture of engagement requires more than completing an annual employee survey and then leaving managers on their own, hoping they will learn something from the survey results that will change their daily behavior. It requires a company to take a close look at the critical engagement elements that align with performance and with the organization's human capital strategy.*

I've had the honor to work with many inspiring leaders in my career, but one in particular demonstrated a distinguishing quality in his day-to-day focus and decision making with astonishing bottom-line results. His secret was to prioritize employee engagement and reiterate this priority to the executive team – ***daily.***

When senior leadership aligns with employee engagement initiatives and makes them a top focus, the business decisions, policies and budget considerations all reflect this alignment.

Identifying what matters most to the employee (your team) via a sound employee engagement survey is a powerful tool if executed with complete autonomy.

When employees are acknowledged as valuable, not from a sweeping gesture but through day-to-day choices and exchanges (and mentoring support), performance skyrockets. Team members contribute in ways that make measurable difference in achieving the organization's goals. Another unsurprising perk to this is having fun while doing it.

Verdict: *The very different and distinguished bring their best with the intent to harmonize in the achievement and experience of a greater vision.*

The Greatness Igniter

On key disciplines of execution:

"Don't get so lost in the WHIRLWIND of activity that you lose sight of your TOP GOALS."

Behavior-changing strategies:

1. Clearly understand the goal to execute. Can you name your organization's top goals? Even one of them?
2. Have passion for the goal you are executing and stay committed to it.
3. Be accountable for achieving the goal and hold others accountable, too.
4. Align goals, foster clarity, build trust and develop processes for good decision making.

Chris McChesney
Greatness Igniter, Co-Author of *The 4 Disciplines of Execution, 4DX*

Wisdom from the Dynamic Visionary

On leading and engaging a dynamic organization successfully:

1. Establish a clear vision supported by a passionate leadership team.
2. Engage team members consistently around that vision.
3. Identify and develop top talent via professional development activities.
4. Consistently communicate the status of top goals throughout the year. Celebrate success!
5. Encourage and reward leaders, team members and teams that exemplify high performance

Phil Goldfarb
Dynamic Visionary, President of legendary South Beach Hotel

Wisdom from The Festive Friend

On forging authentic relationships:

- WELCOME new and different people into your life
- DEMONSTRATE integrity and character
- TREAT people with warmth and kindness
- LIVE with an abundant mentality
- VALUE your roots (Regardless of your success, never forget where you came from)

Bill Mackey
Festive Friend, Director of Information Systems

Intention Four: Engage with Authenticity

1. 60% Honor your nature and identify your strengths
2. 30% Listen to others carefully, notice body language, have compassion
3. 10% Measure with precision, conduct critical conversations and provide behavior-based training

Section **Five**

Align Your Frequency

Your greatest challenge as a leader (and person) may be effectively managing your own energy.

Life can get in the way of establishing good routines, thinking good thoughts, and trusting the whispering voice of our genius that often lies beneath all of the mental noise and clutter of life.

With so many directions and choices, where do you start?

You start with alignment.

But you cannot get to alignment by simply stating it—that is why this section is last.

True alignment comes when you have tested the waters and exposed yourself to new ideas, stories, insights, and perspectives. Each voice has its own unique experiences and stories of success, and they can vary in their approach but all still be successful.

The formula for a great employee engagement outcome is the intention to prepare to win, protect, and build your culture; understand your landscape; engage with integrity; and, now, ALIGN your energy.

Aligning your energy is a powerful last step that must be a priority every single day. This process requires that your heart, mind, and behavior all have ONE unified intention and that you have decided to consciously make decisions in that direction. That direction is the deepest, truest, and most authentic version of:

WHO YOU ARE.

Our frequency can be powerful, attractive, creative, and influential only if we value what we think, feel, and do. It is in this intention that the true distinction occurs between those who superficially attempt to achieve visions and those who actually bring them to life.

Let's explore the following practices to ensure that as a leader, team member, parent, and friend you "manage your frequency particles" and resonate the greatest expression of yourself.

To engage others who are in that same space is where the magic is!

Four Key Practices for Frequency Alignment

1. Find and align your frequency.
2. Think with your head, **know** with your body.
3. Trust resonance, **manage** dissonance.
4. Wait for the DING!

PRACTICE ONE: FIND AND ALIGN YOUR FREQUENCY

...because you cannot fake presence.

Finding and aligning your frequency is about getting to the very core of who you are, what you are passionate about and how you choose to contribute your talents.

When you are aligned, you offer tremendous value. Why? Because no one offers the unique recipe that is you. There is no competition to be you. There is just you. You are the only one. You are that significant. That is, if you are being true to yourself. You can, of course, present an outwardly polished version of yourself, but without internal alignment, this is just window dressing.

Isn't it time we master the skills to effectively collaborate **with fundamentally different people** who also display this heightened personal congruency to make collaborative and meaningful contributions? Can such collaboration solve local and global challenges?

Instead of power struggles, personality clashes and costly communication breakdowns, there would be cooperation, creative solutions and innovation.

Isn't it worth the ***internal work*** to align, and worth the ***external work*** to harmonize?

Simply put: Empowered people perform better.

As an example, an empowered employee being compensated a $60,000 salary can make a greater contribution in one year than an unengaged employee with the same salary over a three-year period who "dials it in." One contributor costs the company $60,000, and the other $180,000 for a ***similar contribution***. The engaged employee represents a $120,000 savings over three years. Not only that, but should the high performer stay for the three years at the same pace of contribution, the ROI far surpasses that of the unengaged individual.

This is not just an economic issue; it is systemic. The unengaged employee settles for a lower standard of life. This can create dissonance and impact workflow, bringing the entire team down.

If this sounds like you as you "go through the motions" due to ineffective senior leadership or outdated and frustrating policies, you may not be living your potential and could be short-changing your life experience.

The good news is, more of us are becoming aligned. We want meaning and purpose. We want to be content, alive and engaged in our worlds. We want to make a positive impact daily.

The bad news is that many companies are at a standstill with employees, still driven by the former system, who have accountability and empowerment preached at them as compensation for said former system but the system itself does not update. It is a catch 22. Even more discouraging are the companies that want unconscious compliance and incur the extensive cost of their unengaged mass or high turnover.

If the "sweet spot" of highly engaged contributors performing well in a growing organization can be achieved, the question of talent retention become a new tension.

Perhaps one response to this natural development can be found in the organically growing group of individuals supplementing their lives with side businesses. These individuals make their meaningful contributions elsewhere, filling the emotional need to align, but it a sort of splintered way.

Is splintering our focus and energy the ideal long-term plan for our lives, communities and organizations? Can organizations truly align (not just in theory) in a way that permeates daily workflow exchanges? This does not mean we do not have multiple interests, as most of us do. It means we must be careful when we seek internal satisfaction from superficial pursuits that leave us depleted – true satisfaction comes only from the alignment of heart, head and skill.

The organizations that do succeed at this rare cocktail of high-performing team members hire well, have a clear vision, communicate clear goals often and build workflows around what they value. Senior leadership in these organizations take employee engagement very seriously. They know the impacts and the results it brings.

An organization with a **state of being** (a quality resonance) attracts, retains and harnesses its likeness to then benefit from the **collective potential of the talented and committed.**

SELF-MANAGEMENT

To be a high performer means you play to your strengths, manage your energy and practice the mental clarity for personal greatness.

Never before in history has self-management been such a critical factor in success. Learning to master your thinking patterns, habits and lifestyle choices is essential in sustaining high performance and enjoying your life in today's diverse and demanding global landscape.

It often breeds a friendlier and more collaborative atmosphere, supportive mentoring, accountability scoreboards and the consistent celebration of success.

Confident contributors have nothing to prove and everything to create.

Add a friendly internal company-wide competition that encourages growth and you have a perfect recipe for sustained excellence and goal achievement.

Self-management is about doing the internal work to be able to come to the table at this level of the playing field. In addition, the ROI on investing in your own brand of genius over your weakness is obvious. This does not imply we dismiss the value of being well-rounded and richly educated; it means we do not drop thousands on a tree-climbing PhD for a fish.

For example, I started my speaking career at 25, and by 27, I had groups as large as 500 giving standing ovations. I had little experience. My stating this is not to boast or gloss over the many failures and learning opportunities I collected over 20 years, but rather to illustrate the power of investing in natural talents.

Not being seasoned can have a cost at times. We rely on mentors to guide us. I recall at one of my well-attended seminars, a "seminar evaluator" came to the event to offer me delivery feedback. It made me very nervous, but I decided to do what I do best.

At the close of the program, before I got to see the 117 evaluations collected, this evaluator quite directly told me I was too short to be a professional speaker.

Just like that. Too short.

She then went on to explain how my hair was not "sophisticated" enough to send a polished message (it was a bob); a French Twist would be much better (I can't make this stuff up).

She also told me I needed to make big, sweeping hand gestures to help the back of the room SEE ME because my petite frame was so inadequate. I imagined this unnatural flapping bird with a nest-like hairstyle. French Twists are tricky with short hair. As I listened to everything she said, I started questioning my appearance, ability to influence an audience and career track as a professional speaker. After all, she was experienced, and I took feedback seriously.

My very impressionable brain went into an insecurity tail spin. I overlooked a critical point: how detrimental unproductive feedback can be to improvement.

Then I read the evaluations.

Most were 10 out of 10 on all measured points – including appearance. I was short, had simple hair and had chosen to walk through the big audience to connect instead of the suggested bird-like performance with sweeping arm movements. According to the data, my sure-to-fail approach worked just fine.

Senior leaders do this to employees everyday. Middle managers do this to talented employees routinely.

Unskillful feedback, even with the best intentions, can crush the mojo right out of talent. I was lucky – I was holding over 100 pieces of paper that said my delivery style was effective. Had I not had this immediate reinforcement, however, I would have gone on her feedback alone and my personal presence would have been squashed – the most critical factor in influencing an audience.

Our innate gifts (when identified and developed) allow us to contribute in immeasurable ways to those around us. We become less about *our* lives and more about the *value* we offer other people's lives.

This does not downplay the incredible advantage of receiving well thought-out critical feedback, but ineffective feedback is damaging.

SELF-MANAGEMENT AND THE PERFORMANCE REVIEW

The performance reviews of today offer feedback, but do little to assist in the complex judgement calls most of us make on a daily basis that carry consequences.

That said, self-management without effective feedback can disperse valuable energy and is costly for both contributor and organization.

Five Keys to an Effective Performance Review:

1. Top goals are made clear.
2. Expected behaviors are clearly stated.
3. Quality training and the tools needed to achieve goals are made available.
4. Daily and weekly feedback loops are constructive and balanced, not destructive or demoralizing (mentors work!).
5. A tracking system for compliance and a routine celebration habit are in place.

When a high performer stops winning, they will simply win elsewhere.

PRACTICE TWO: THINK WITH YOUR HEAD, KNOW WITH YOUR BODY

How do you *know with your body* when your *head* does all the thinking?

Have you ever found yourself overthinking something to the point that you lose clarity? Has a restless mind kept you from sleeping or a "to do" list become your whole life?

Many of us have these experiences from time to time. We let our minds drive our lives, then ask our bodies to catch up. We grab the comfort food, skip sleep and ignore critical hunches for less-than-ideal consequences.

It is important that we recognize and respect our bodies as true communication tools. The body communicates with us all the time. Many of the most famous and successful people attribute their best decisions to gut instincts and hunches. These hunches are pulls or pushes toward or away from someone or something as discerned by the body.

I recall as a teenager taking a trip to New York City with my best friend. We were well prepared with maps and took a train from New Jersey into the city for a day of fun.

While walking around and enjoying the visual stimulation, I noticed a man come out of a man hole and walk toward us. I did not think too much about it, so we kept walking.

Then my body got a very uneasy feeling. I ignored it, assuming it was big city jitters.

It would not go away.

The uneasiness would not cease, so I decided to apply my mind to figure it out.

Decision one: I looked behind us to see the man following us slowly.

Mind over body: My mind said, "Oh he just happens to be walking in this direction". My body said, "Be wary".

Decision two: I ignored the uneasy feeling and kept walking.

Body over mind: The uneasy feeling got stronger and more uncomfortable.

Decision three: I asked my friend to behave normally, as if talking to me about the city, as I tested something that was bothering me. A true comrade and trusted friend, she jumped into character and played "two teenagers enjoying the big city."

Decision four: I jay-walked. He jay-walked.

Decision five: I crossed the street. He crossed the street.

Decision six: I backtracked and crossed back to the original street. He followed.

Mind and Body: "This man is most certainly following us. We are vulnerable and need a safe place to go."

Decision seven: Walk swiftly into a big toy store and go to the security office.

Mind over Body: The elevator was the only way up to security and the crowd was too heavy to see if he had followed us in. I told myself, "I think we are safe and he gave up."

Decision eight: My friend and I pretended like she was looking and talking about a toy on a nearby isle as a diversion. As her voice placed us in the isle, I checked the elevator and surrounding area. It was clear. I waved to her to get in quickly to head to security. We both hurried into the elevator and pushed the button to go.

Body, no Mind: He jumped in **out of nowhere** and I screamed so loudly that I think all the floors in the store heard. He jumped out and ran away.

Mind and Body: Thank you both.

The more we make quality decisions based on our instincts and our ability to discern beyond mental deliberation, the more effective we become overall. Think with your head but KNOW with your body, even if it takes some time to merge them.

It is worth the practice.

Every time a persistent uneasy feeling surfaces, question it. It may not always mean a lurking stranger, but it usually means something.

Think with your head. *Know* with your body.

PRACTICE THREE: TRUST RESONANCE, MANAGE DISSONANCE

Trust is also linked to self-management.

Trust does not come from risk or chance; it is incrementally built. It is established by observing consistency. Consistency in behavior creates trust. We work faster and more effectively with trust. We trust ourselves more with experience. Our trial and error "data bank" offers us probability trajectories to choose from to determine results with greater accuracy.

When a practice shows consistent results, we trust that practice.

When a brand name delivers consistently high quality, we purchase with less evaluation.

Trust is confidence.

Trust is the belief that what you expect will show up.

Self-trust is everything in a confusing and distracting world, as is discernment.

But how does one achieve self-trust? The kind of trust that will enable you to take risks?

One word: Practice.

One afternoon at a children's hospital, I was greeted by a dramatic domestic outburst between two parents in one of the outpatient care areas. A father was trying to see his child at the hospital, but a restraining order was in place by the mother. Emotions were running high and the situation worsening.

With a clipboard in hand from the previous orientation session, I walked the hall toward the commotion. Personally, I was quite centered and relaxed. Alert even.

Looking around, I noticed no one was responding to the escalating drama.

There were no calls being made, no security in the area and people were pulling their children out of the way. I realized I was the only leader to appear at the scene.

Then I saw it. A gun neatly tucked into the pants of the man screaming and yelling as his hand flirted with the touch–release toggle.

The argument got louder, and people started to duck behind walls.

Still unclear on how to respond, I decided I needed to do *something*. I walked up to the aggressive man and asked, "Are you ok, sir?"

He kept yelling. I agreed with him. I had no idea what he said, but I agreed.

He yelled some more. I agreed some more. My instincts (body) told me to agree, so I kept agreeing.

Over and over he yelled about how upset he was, how unfair it was, how angry he was – and I just agreed and validated every single one of his feelings. As I was agreeing, I started to stroll. He followed me.

We walked together slowly, resembling a weird window shopping scene, as if two old friends were taking a walk with coffees and witty banter.

He followed me right to the outpatient exit area of the hospital. With each slow step, he calmed down a little more.

I casually suggested that we get some air, and asked him respectfully if we could go outside. He agreed.

By the time we were outside, he broke down in tears, offering that he was "not normally like this". I felt compassion creep through the wall of adrenaline that had been racing through my body. He was a person with feelings. A dangerous person, but a person.

The police arrived. I felt tremendous relief.

As I walked back into the building, my body started to shake uncontrollably. I saw fellow colleagues nod at me, saying thank you. I walked straight into the restroom, still shaking, and broke down.

Apparently, I had "forgotten" to be terrified and was now giving myself the space to process what had just happened.

Verdict: Telling an emotionally reactive person to "calm down" could trigger an escalation.

Sometimes we practice self-trust in the small risks we take that give us good outcomes and greater confidence. Sometimes we trust that something larger, more mysterious and profound guides our lives for a higher purpose.

I do not recommend this kind of action to others as it was a purely personal choice based on unique intuition that only I could sense at the time.

What I *do* recommend is to develop clear, established safety procedures and trainings.

Panic and more drama would not have been productive in that particular moment.

ORGANIZATIONS, LEADERS AND EMPLOYEES ARE MADE UP OF **PEOPLE**.

An organization is comprised of different work styles, values and personalities. Organizations (and families) are made up of people.

What triggers behavior the most?

EMOTIONS.

How Emotions (feelings) Influence:

- HR studies show that many employees quit their jobs because of their immediate supervisors.
- Most sales and marketing gurus will tell you that emotion-backed communication sells.
- One person can negatively impact the morale of an entire team (known as the "bad apple" example).
- We make bad decisions when we are emotionally upset.
- Customers make most buying decisions based on emotions.
- Most relationships (personal, teams or families) are emotional connections.

This is not to suggest we lower our expectations, performance standards or avoid holding others accountable to safeguard emotions;

what it does mean is that emotional impact is worth considering when the goal is to create a harmonic and successful environment.

Leaders that have influence usually have an ability **to maintain positive and encouraging emotions themselves and can set a consistent tone.**

This is important when nurturing a learning environment. A learning mindset is the path to personal development and self-management. Positive feelings can be in the form of encouragement, enthusiasm, collaborative language or a friendly disposition.

FACT:

Maintaining positive feelings takes consistent focus and practice to rewire our brains and garner results.

PRACTICE FOUR: WAIT FOR THE "DING!"

What do I mean, "The DING?"

Have you ever attempted to cut corners in your work and later felt that the diluted effort cost you? Have you ever found yourself deliberating a decision in your mind repeatedly, then suddenly you hear, see or remember something and BOOM, you have *clarity?* Have you ever compromised, backed-down or made excuses for something only to learn later that . . .

YOU DID NOT WAIT FOR THE DING!

That FEELING of certainty, knowing, clarity, confidence and alignment.

When your head, heart and body ALIGN and say **YES!**

That is the **DING!**

Too many of us don't wait for it and end up wasting time, energy and resources on a decision, direction or relationship that **has more dissonance then resonance.**

Now, this absolutely does not mean you do not execute due diligence, ask questions, get references or gather important critical data; what it does mean is that when we feel that deep internal ding before moving forward, we might just find we make:

BETTER DECISIONS

and have

BETTER RELATIONSHIPS

and join

BETTER TEAMS

and buy

BETTER PRODUCTS AND SERVICES

and accomplish

BIG DREAMS.

To think with your head and know with your body comes to a full circle with the DING.

Listening to the DING is worth practicing every single day until you fully trust yourself.

Intention Five: Align Your Frequency

RECIPE FOR ALIGNING YOUR FREQUENCY

1. 70% Discover and express your passions, talents and strengths
2. 20% Practice your passions
3. 10% Put yourself in uncomfortable situations to grow

SELF-CARE CLOSING
… because if you exhaust yourself, you can't engage.

Have you ever been tired, depleted and in no mood to be pleasant? Maybe you did not sleep or personal stressors impacted you. The cause of the mojo leak doesn't matter; it is our responsibility to plug it.

To perform well and consistently, you must prioritize your energy. Powerful morning routines, meditation, ice baths, exercise and quality nutrition are the common practices of some of the most influential and successful people in our world.

We can learn from others, do our own research or establish the routines that resonate best with own natures. Determining how to take responsibility for a high or low vibe is not as important as actually doing it – ***daily.***

It is very important that to maintain your wellbeing, especially if you are in the throes of your own Hero's Journey, you make it a top personal goal. Without mojo you cannot conquer the dragons, climb the mountains or achieve your goals.

Your Frequency Matters.

Our final three voices share their insights into avoiding burnout, feeling happier, and opening your heart to life. Above all, take care of yourself each and every day so that you have the ENERGY to take care of others.

From the Lifestyle Luminaire

On avoiding burnout:

NUTRITION

Step 1 - Eat wholesome foods.

Step 2 - Drink water.

Step 3 - Get moving.

Step 4 - Indulge in a spiritual practice.

Step 5 - Eat mindfully with attention and presence.

Shahnaz Nensey
Lifestyle Luminaire, Board Certified Doctor of Natural Medicine

Inspiration from the Body Balancer

- Make your health a priority.

- Keep your workouts fresh and your body guessing – *you can modify any exercise.*

- Set small, realistic goals (e.g., complete a 5K run or execute 10 push-ups). Once you've achieved them, set new ones.

- Never say "I can't!" – YOU CAN and YOU WILL!

- No fancy gym equipment needed. Think outside the box.

- Consistency is key; aim for 3–4 workouts per week.

- Calories taken in should be less than or equal to calories burned.

Andi Burbank
Body Balancer, Personal Trainer and Fitness Expert

From the Frequency Adjustor
On happiness:

> "Choose to live a drama-free life and love and accept yourself for who you are right now. A happy heart shifts energy in amazing ways."

Roxanne Smith
Frequency Adjustor, LaHoChi Teacher/Practioner

The Love Lady
On Compassion:

Above everything is Love. Not the fairytale and puppy kind of love, but *real* love found in the thought and care of another being with nothing to gain for ourselves. Directing that positive and piercing emotion to another being, whether they know or even want it, should be our aim in life.

This applies to every part of our lives, not just the "big" moments. Aim to walk the walk 24 hours a day, 7 days a week. A good person doesn't act like a good person sometimes or when others are looking; a good person IS a good person all the time.

When (not if) you fail, this doesn't mean you're a bad person – it means you dust off the dirt and proudly show what you've survived.

When (not if) others fail, it doesn't mean they're bad people – it just means they're people. LOVE them and help them get up. Show them that they can be proud of what they've lived through.

Repeat.

Samantha Wheatly
Love Lady, Human Resources Executive

"Always, always about love. And when it is not about love, it is then MOST about love."

- Robert Brian Lalena, Elementary School Teacher

Find and align your own frequency; think with your head, *know* with your body; trust resonance, *manage* dissonance; and wait for the DING!

...then MAKE YOUR ENERGY YOUR PRIORITY.

SUMMARY:

Intention One: **Prepare to Win**
Intention Two: **Influence Your Landscape**
Intention Three: **Define and Refine your Culture**
Intention Four: **Engage with Authenticity**
Intention Five: **Align your Frequency**

Intention One: **Prepare to Win**

RECIPE FOR WINNING

1. 50% Alignment with passions, gifts, talents and strengths
2. 25% Mental focus
3. 25% Consistent practice of an aligned heart and mind

Intention Two: **Influence Your Landscape**

RECIPE FOR A LANDSCAPE

1. 60% Passionate alignment with the landscape (industry, craft, lifestyle, work).
2. 20% Learn how to become an effective contributor within the landscape.
3. 20% Maintain a learning mindset and adapt skillfully.

Intention Three: **Define and Refine your Culture**

RECIPE FOR CULTURE

1. 90% Leadership-driven and supported
2. 5% Rock star performers set the bar
3. 5% Train and support the rock stars to be the next leaders

Intention Four: **Engage with Authenticity**

RECIPE FOR ENGAGING WITH AUTHENTICITY

1. 50% Measure with precision, seek expertise and conduct critical conversations.
2. 25% Determine what behaviors correlate with established outcomes.
3. 25% Provide behavior-based training to enhance high-correlation behaviors.

Intention Five: **Align Your Frequency**

RECIPE FOR ALIGNING YOUR FREQUENCY

1. 70% Discover and express your passions, talents and strengths.
2. 20% Practice your passions.
3. 10% Put yourself in uncomfortable situations to grow.

Feel Good. Do Good. Have Fun.
The Meaningful Contribution

We must create a lifestyle of wellbeing for true greatness to flourish.

A lifestyle of wellbeing is not a lifestyle of leisure, nor is it laced with struggle and strain; rather it is found in establishing authentic connections and making meaningful contributions.

It is about the "others" in our lives (whether family or not) where true fulfillment lies – not to the determent of self, but the expansion.

Profound meaning can be in the experience of watching greatness unfold as you see and accept the world as it was meant to be – diverse and beautiful.

Profound meaning can be in the person you just mentored, the company you built, the people's lives you influenced because you were committed to your vision.

Profound meaning can be in the daily choices you make that inspire others; the humor, attitude, gestures, strategies and solutions; or the grace you teach your children every day.

Profound meaning can be found in coaching or transforming a team, igniting someone's potential or making things better with your honest and accurate assessment – because truth is essential to greatness.

Profound meaning can be in the mistakes you fixed, the lessons you learned, the risks you took that made you wiser, smarter and more yourself than ever before.

It can be in the board meeting you influence, the idea you present, the process you improve or the creative idea you launch.

It is found in the meal you mindfully craft or the food you beautifully grow or the muscles you consistently build both physically and conceptually.

What makes something profound is the recognition that living from the heart yields dividends far beyond what the mind can calculate.

And being part of something larger then yourself is what makes life worthwhile.

Uniquely together, in harmony.

It is the realization that goodness was not the exception but the rule, and that when it comes to true, effective, powerful and purposeful engagement, what yields the outcomes we as people, leaders, parents and friends strive for?

Frequency Matters.

REFLECTION SECTION

This section a space for you to collect ideas and jot down insights.

NOTE-TAKING PROMPTS

The Bubbles = flurries of thoughts and ideas – **the NEW**

The Cubes = organized thoughts and ideas – **the CLARIFIED or DECIDED**

The Practice = embodiment of thoughts and ideas into form – **the FREQUENCY**

Kristin Mackey

"Draw your life with a pencil to safely erase mistakes, or draw your life with a pen to show the courage that it takes."

Kristin is a highly sought-after motivational speaker and author of two books, You Can, You Will, You Did; Micro Changes for Macro Transformation *and* Frequency Matters. *She is known for her high energy and engaging style of delivery with easy-to-implement techniques.*

Kristin was recognized by Training Magazine *as "One to Watch" and has appeared on The Balancing Act/Lifetime TV, EmpoweredKidsTV and in The Washington Times' Community section. As a consultant for FranklinCovey for over 10 years, she facilitated several key programs, including* The 7 Habits of Highly Effective People. *She is currently a speaker for FranklinCovey Speakers Bureau.*

As a keynote speaker, she speaks to groups ranging from hundreds to several thousands and works with companies such as Lockheed Martin, Mercury Media, Laura Mercier, The Department of Safety and Homeland Security, Hardrock Casino and Resort, Tyco, PricewaterhouseCoopers, the City of Miami Beach and several universities.

Kristin lives in Florida with her husband Paul and enjoys running, cartoon illustration, meditation and travel. She adores her family, including eight beloved nieces, and has friends worldwide.

kristinmackey.com

Shawn Herbig

"Let your interests and passions guide you in the questions that you ask, but keep those same interests and passions out of the answers that you form."

In his current role, Shawn is the President and Founder of IQS Research. During his tenure, he has designed and overseen hundreds of research projects, ranging from small qualitative studies involving only a handful of high-value respondents to projects interviewing several thousand respondents, conducted in multiple languages and across numerous continents.

Shawn hails from the automotive industry where he started as an evaluator for prototype vehicles before becoming the Quality Analyst and ultimately Lead Quality Analyst for the Ford Explorer vehicle line. He has developed his knowledge base to include myriad feedback and analysis tools in the areas of consumer, market and employee research.

An avid reader of non-fiction, Shawn enjoys spending time outdoors and running through the many parks in Louisville, Kentucky. He is happily married to his wife, Kathy, and has been for over 22 years. He has two stepsons, Shawn and Michael.

http://iqsresearch.com

REFERENCES

Berlinger, J., Wilkes, J., Koppelman, B., Levien, D., Huffman, K., Gray, L. (Producers), & Berlinger, J. (Director). (2016). *Tony Robbins: I am not your guru* [Documentary]. US: Joe Berlinger Films.

Blanchard, K. H. (2010). *Leading at a higher level: Blanchard on leadership and creating high performing organizations.* Upper Saddle River, NJ: FT Press.

Blanchard, K. H., & Shula, D. (2001). *The little book of coaching: motivating people to be winners.* New York, NY: HarperBusiness.

Campbell, J., & Cousineau, P. (2014). *The hero's journey: Joseph Campbell on his life and work.* Novato, CA: New World Library.

Covey, S. R. (2009). *Focus: Achieving your highest priorities the new workshop to help you focus on and execute top priorities.* Salt Lake City, UT: Franklin Covey Company, GABAL.

Covey, S. R., & Covey, F. (1998). *The 7 habits of highly effective people.*

Salt Lake City, UT: Franklin Covey Company.

Mackey, K. (2012). *You can, you will, you did.* Bloomington, IN: Balboa Press.

Robbins, A. (1992). *Awaken the giant within: How to take immediate control of your mental, emotional, physical and financial distiny.* New York: Simon & Schuster.

McChesney, C., Covey, S., & Huling, J. (2016). *The 4 disciplines of execution: achieving your wildly important goals.* New York, NY: Free Press.

Sabbag, M. (2009). *Developing exemplary performance one person at a time.* Boston, MA and Clerkenwell, London: Davies-Black, an imprint of Nicholas Brealey Publishing.

Sibley, B. (2001). *The Lord of the Rings official movie guide.* Boston, MA: Houghton Mifflin.

RESOURCES

Kristin Mackey
Professional Speaker and Author/artist for KMack®
kristinmackey.com
office: 800-632-1752
kristin@kristinmackey.com

Shawn Herbig
President and Founder IQS Research
www.iqsresearch.com
office: 502-244-6600
sherbig@iqsresearch.com

Cheryl Arpa, MSW, LSW
Licensed School Board Counselor
www.linkedin.com/in/cheryl-arpa-msw-lsw

Scott Baker
Head Men's Soccer Coach
Rowan University
http://www.rowanuniversitysoccercamps.com

Peter T. Boyd, Esq
General Guru
Paperstreet Web Design
www.paperstreet.com

Andi Burbank
Personal Trainer and Fitness Expert
andiburbank@gmail.com

Eric S. Czerniejewski, P.E., ENV SP
President, Infrastructure & Mobility Transportation Consultants, LLC
www.infrastructuremobility.com
eczerniejewski@gmail.com

David Haskins
Research and Development Professional
davidehaskins@aol.com
www.linkedin.com/in/davidehaskins

Jeffrey Keller, MS, MBA
Vice President Strategic Partnerships Priority 1 Signs
www.p1signs.com
jkeller@p1signs.com

Maggie Macaulay, MS Ed
President of WholeHearted Parenting
www.WholeHeartedParenting.com
maggie_macaulay@msn.com

Bill Mackey
Information Systems Expert Consultant
wmackey22@gmail.com

Shahnaz Nensey
Board Certified Doctor of Natural Medicine
www.Shahnaz.life
shahnaz@shahnaz.life.com

Lori Riordan
Partner, Human Resources Consultant
LGR Consulting
linkedin.com/in/lori-g-riordan

Michael Sabbag
Executive, Speaker, Author
www.michaelsabbag.com

Roxanne Smith
LaHoChi Teacher/Practitioner
www.theharmoniousheart.com
info@theharmoniousheart.com

Contact Kristin Mackey@:
kristinmackey.com
kristin@kristinmackey.com
800-632-1752

Contact Shawn Herbig@:
iqsresearch.com
sherbig@iqsresearch.com
502-244-6600

ACKNOWLEDGMENTS

To my husband, Paul, for your love, support and friendship. My life's work would not be possible without you. Thank you for everything.

To Shawn Herbig, Founder of IQS Research, for your brilliance, attention to detail, commitment and insightful candor.

A special thank you to Peter Boyd, "General Guru" and the Paperstreet Web Design team for your endless support, inspiring talent and the immeasurable contributions you have made to my work.

A special thank you to each and every voice presented in this book. My deepest and sincere gratitude for your willingness, wisdom and participation in this collective contribution. You are each an inspiration:

Chris Mcchesney, Shawn Herbig, Pete Boyd, Philip Goldfarb, Michael Sabbag, Jeffrey Keller, Bill Mackey, Cheryl Arpa, Scott Baker, Jackie Reeves, Scott DiGerolamo, Shahnaz Nensey, Roxanne Smith, Andi Burbank, David Haskins, Jill Straffi, Lori Riordan, Samantha Wheatly, Rosavel Trujillo, Rosaya Trujillo, Maggie MaCaulay, Eric Czerniejewski.

A sincere thank you to Dave Arpa for his warm and empathic frequency and to Kristin-Jones Mackey (KJ) for the depth of wisdom you carry in your loving and humorous frequency. You are both beautiful and valued. And to the wonderful and loved DiObilda family, thank you.

To my sensitive, uplifting, intelligent, warm and fun nieces (in order of age): Caroline, Nikki, Cassadie, Courtney, Nina, Lucy, Nora and my "soon-to-be" new angel — I love you.

An acknowledgment to my inspiring and hilarious dear friend, David Haskins. Your strength, wisdom and gentle push made this book possible. Whip it! Thank you for always being there.

Emmanuel Toku-White – you transcend distance as a source of goodness; thank you.

A heartfelt and sincere thank you to the FranklinCovey family. Since 2006, you have positively influenced my life and work by your example as professionals, the incredible content you offer and the principles to which you anchor and live by.

Thank you Jason Weissman for your expertise, insight and friendship.

A warm and sincere thank you to the following "frequencies" who made this work possible:

My dearly loved entire extended family – **all of you, including those dearly missed.** St. Joseph High School, Alice H., Karen M., David T., Barb M., Jennifer C., Hoover, Joey P., (Lou forever), Geraldine, Dorthy Cartica, Maddy Gold, Danielle Batten, Robert Brian Lalena, Rowan University, Sandy Thurston, Anthony Iacobone, Kara Travis, Terri Young (Starfish), Pat Alexy-Stoll (w/Nick DiObilda), Marylyn Nyman, Emily and Jason Braham, Caroline W., Jamie B., FranklinCovey, JuneBug and Bev, Balboa Press, Gwen Fuller, Goodtastic Productions, Jessica Ganson, Cindy Mason, Andrew Mackey, Crystal Capone, Kendra Alyse Bollenbach, Bill Penn, Keith Wescoat, Marni Henry-Parks, Karen Namiotcavage Ciotti, Phoebe Chan, Mike Schwager, Sloan Folsom Robocker, Diane Estevez, Ben DiObilda, Joveline J. Pettus, Marni Arnason, Pamela Alaina-Marie, Lorraine DiStefano, Lisa Hatcher, Shirah Penn, William Jason Omara, Bert, Laslo Vanger, Christian Hidalgo, Mary Oxley.

"Frequencies are as unique as fingerprints; each one tells us exclusive information to expand our own potential."
- Rosaya Trujillo

NOTES

NOTES

NOTES

NOTES

NOTES

NOTES

Made in the USA
Columbia, SC
06 January 2018